Sanda Nitesco

A SPRIG OF DILL

A Memoir flavoured with Romanian cuisine

Published in the United Kingdom by
Pholiota Publications
British Library Cataloguing in Publication Data available
ISBN 978-0-9554627-02

First published July, 2007

Designer: David Tsai, www.DavidTsai.co.uk
Printed and bound in the United Kingdom

Pholiota Publications, a division of American Eyes Ltd.
197 Kings Cross Road
London WC1X 9DB
Tel: 020 7278 9490
www.americanization.com

ACKNOWLEDGEMENTS AND DEDICATION

The author would like to thank the following for their assistance: Françoise Agratina, Mircea Anghelescu, Elena Avram, Rosy and Paul Barbanegra, Rodica Binder, Serban Cristovici, Vasile Igna, Imprimerie Point 16, Mariana Ioan, Gaby Ionesco, Brice Matthieussent, Mariana Net, Gil de Poncheville, Alexandru Vona, Micrea Zacui, Katarzyna Zelaska and Florence Chevallard.

The translator and publisher would like to thank Anca Mocan who so assiduously read the text and gave advice on Romanian spellings and other matters and Laura Bol for her proofreading. Thanks are also due to Calin Itoaie of Baia Mare, Romania and Chris of the Romanian Restaurant at 32 Old Bailey, London, England for their enormous help with photographic illustrations.

This translation is dedicated to the memory of Bogdan Chirila (1961–2007).

'Without my having to produce any new reasoning, find any decisive arrangement, my difficulties, insoluble at any time, had lost any importance that they might have had. But this time I had decided not to resign myself to failing to understand why, as I had done on the day I tasted a madeleine dipped in herb tea. The felicity I had just experienced was indeed the same as upon eating the madeleine but I had delayed it in order to seek out the most profound reasons for it.'

Marcel Proust, *Time Regained*

CONTENTS
Page

1

ABOUT THE ROMANIAN WORDS IN THE TEXT

In the original text, the author tried to reproduce the sound of the Romanian words – mostly the names of dishes or places – using an approximately equivalent French pronunciation. Since Romanian pronunciation and spellings are even more remote from English than from French, the actual Romanian spellings of these words have been used and a glossary and pronunciation guide are provided at the end of the book.

TRANSLATOR'S INTRODUCTION

When I first came across this book, I was enchanted by the author's evocative style and vivid depictions of her life in Romania. I discovered it through the author's son, Vladimir, who was studying in London and showed me the book when he came to my translation company for work experience. I sincerely hope I have done justice to the author's magically evocative style, and that the reader will forgive me if she or he feels that I have not adequately conveyed the spirit of the original.

This is the third book I have published, the first under the name of Pholiota Publications; the other two were published by Pholiota Press in Garden Grove, California. Like the previous two books, 'The Jewish Cookery Book' and 'The Jews of Poland: Recipes and Recollections' the subject is cookery-related. Had I sought a commercial publisher for the previous books and this one, my discoveries would probably have been rejected out of hand. An agent to whom I mentioned this book commented, 'Oh, it's about cooking. Do people still cook?' Either way, I feared rejection ('It's very good but it's not for us') or – worse still – having it accepted for publication only to discover that the publisher had decided to commission someone else to translate it. After all, I had no legal

2

rights to any credit or acknowledgement. Even had the publisher reluctantly decided to 'take a chance' on the book and even commission the translation from me, the remuneration I would have been offered would have been minimal and I would not have been granted any rights unless I waived my fee altogether. Having worked for many years in publishing, I am familiar with the methodology.

I also wanted to be sure of having complete control of the design and layout. A previous cookery book I wrote, published by a large commercial publisher, was so badly laid out that in some cases the recipe titles appear on the page preceding the actual recipe. In another of my books, 'Patisserie of Vienna', an impossibly elaborate, iced and decorated cake was used as the cover picture, instead of the plain *gugelhupf* sprinkled with a little sifted icing sugar that I had recommended. This conveyed the very opposite of the message that I intended to convey, namely that Viennese home baking can be simple and the results delicious. Another book – not a cookery book – that I produced for a large publisher, who demanded the copyright and has sold the book in huge quantities, was unsympathetically edited by a desk editor who was totally unfamiliar with the subject. Furthermore, the introduction was written by someone whose political views are completely at odds with my own.

'A Sprig of Dill' is also an opportunity for me in the forty-sixth year of my translation career to escape for an instant from the dreary texts that keep a translator from the breadline: contracts of sale, the rules of navigation, building regulations, reports and accounts and an endless series of writs and subpoenas, judgements and statements of claim. Despite having translated a large number of books from both French and Hebrew – nearly a book a month in some years – almost all of them have been cookery or art books. This memoir, while still including the food and recipes which are part of my expertise, gives me the opportunity to translate a literary text of great beauty that fills me with enthusiasm. I hope it will be enjoyed just as much by other readers.

JOSEPHINE BACON

3

Dreams and memories
First letter to Agnes

S ometimes I have dreams that recur at intervals. They obsess me, they seem to want to take me over, woven as they are from key images, presented like the playing-cards in a game that forces me to unravel some long-forgotten secret. Look, here's one that's absolutely fresh, hot from my bed, I will tell you the dream before I have had time to forget it. I have had it several times, I have almost succeeded in triggering it myself.

I am in a house that is like a composite of the various homes I have had during the course of my nomadic existence as an exile. But by over-dressing it like an elaborate stage set, it reveals that glorious form of disorder which I describe as 'creative'. As if on a battlefield, but larger than life, huge mounds of books are scattered here and there amid crushed biscuits and cracked vases containing withered foliage. Sketchpads and paintbrushes, laid down for a moment beside a badly dented copper pot, highlight the brilliant hues of the Turkish and Persian carpets and the embroidered cushions that have been visited mercilessly by the claws of my cats – on rickety sideboards, half-eaten apples slumber in old fruit-bowls.

From the midst of this inextricable mess there rises a large, oval table, clean, neat and beautifully laid with an immaculate cloth, in sharp contrast to the surrounding devastation by which it appears to be unaffected. Dear friends are seated around this table and there is a festive atmosphere that is fairly solemn without being too formal; here are the faces of the various acquaintances I have collected in the course of these years of separation, of estrangement, through all my wanderings, traversed with bitterness and joy, with malice and torment, a prey to the vertigo caused by falling from a great height. These are the witnesses to the ecstasy, the many tears, the hand-to-hand combat and frenzied whirl of the dance...

This colourful little group contains representatives of every nation — Japanese, English, American, Dutch, even Argentine — as well as Romanian. All of them look serene, at peace, bonded by a sort of tacit understanding.

In the very centre of the table there sits a giant *mămăligă*, hot, golden and smoking, billowing clouds of steam. The diners are seated in a circle and, as if united by the effect of a mysterious current, accept, inhale and seem to be suffused with the benevolent blandness of the *mămăligă*, smiling beatifically as if experiencing a sort of ecstasy. They appear to be deep in contemplative expectation.

Suddenly, as if sensing a miracle, all heads turn towards a distant corner of the room. At the back, from the doorway to the little kitchen – which reveals itself to be the kitchen of our old flat in Bucharest – a plump little woman emerges. She holds herself erect, as if ceremonially. With a proud gesture that I recognise, she presents an offering, a heavy, lidded cooking-pot that emits a deliciously warm fragrance, the sublime aroma of *sarmale*.

It is Esti, radiating a light that seems to come from within her; she is wearing the flower-sprigged dress she keeps for special occasions, so overwhelmed is she at the opportunity of waiting on these *musafiri* who have come from so far away.

To perpetuate. Permanence. Losing oneself in order to rediscover oneself the better. Transmigrating across frontiers. Ever since I lost and found myself again, on another plane, fallen from the nest and launched into a dizzying sprint, hurtling through strange countries, leaping strange barriers, each time only inches from the abyss until I reached 'the point of no return', shouting at the top of my voice from amidst the maelstrom that was bearing me away, I have always grasped at these roots that have never left me and, to an ever-increasing extent, I have felt their sweet power from somewhere deep within myself, in my heart and in my veins.

When I meet other Romanians who, like me, are scattered throughout the world, and whom I have encountered on my travels through other countries, Germany, the United States, Holland and Spain, I see on their faces the features of a shared past life that I never noticed when I was still in Romania, more than a quarter of a century ago.

Beyond any discord, any misunderstanding, above all beyond any distancing, although perhaps as a result of it, it was through the food we share that we have been able to evoke our common origin. Through food, we are still able to get together, at least for the time it takes to eat a meal. During these meetings, we are able to discover the indestructible bonds that bind us to each other; there is the same nostalgia, the same pain, that visceral void that tears a person apart when far from a loved one or a beloved place, that longing, the homesickness that smothers a cry from deep within us and that bears the Romanian name of *dor*.

Even if we do not share the same opinions, the same obsessions, I have noticed that our sense of smell and our tastebuds are super-sensitive to the aromas, odours and flavours that cradled us from earliest childhood; the fragrance of *borş*, the intoxicating smell of *musaka*, the olfactory ecstasy that we experience when peppers are being grilled in the kitchen... And of course, they include the warm, intimate sensation provided by *mămăligă* or a copious dish of *sarmale* impregnated with fragrant spices, a sensation that comes from the depths of the soul. All these are echoes from our shared fantasy world, an intangible universe but one that is incorrigibly Romanian.

I also realised that, just like me, these Romanians who had dispersed all over the place also loved to communicate our culinary practices to their adopted compatriots, an identity into which such similar tastes and smells are kneaded, and that is now clothed in an aura of nobility that distance had procured for them. Placed from the outset on a pedestal, sublimated with the passing of time, Romanian cuisine penetrates the most secret orifice of my spirit until it even invades my dreams.

So that is the still-fresh, still-warm dream I wanted to share with you. It is one of those 'key-dreams' that I occasionally have, bearing some message that has reached me from a long way away.

In the Thrall of *Dor*, that typically Romanian Sentiment

Second letter to Agnes

What can one say about these endless rainy days?... It is so depressing to watch the windows covered in a tearful veil of rain droplets, the greyness of the sky in the height of summer while, outside, gusts of wind continually shake the foliage in the garden opposite. The rigid structures of La Défense melt into the horizon, a threatening, dominating solid block, advancing like a battalion on the attack.

When this sort of weather obstinately sets in, I apply myself to writing. I am unshakeable, I choose another form of happiness. In fact, I always have a little store of happiness in reserve somewhere close. How else could I survive?

The endless road of exile... It was in those long-ago beginnings that we met each other for the first time. I had just landed from my native Romania. I was a painter and had managed, with great difficulty, to acquire an exit visa, thanks to a scholarship I had been awarded by the French government. The people surrounding me regarded me as if I were some strange object that they were unable to pigeonhole and it took a long time for me to really assimilate. I was excited by this initial, long-awaited excursion into the 'free world' of the West, and rather badly dressed. Before my departure I had managed to procure, not without some difficulty and on the black market, a cardboard suitcase and an 'off-white' fake fur coat which I had naïvely confused with the attributes of elegance.

9

Once in Paris, at first I clung close to the walls and, even in the streets, I spoke softly, always feeling that I was being followed, spied upon. I realised to what extent the imprint left by so many years lived under the yoke of a totalitarian regime had reached the dimensions of a veritable psychosis. When seated on a café terrace I would feel naked, exposed to indiscreet glances; I was blinded by the bright glare of the lights of the Champs Elysées and the red tablecloths that covered the bistro tables were all too reminiscent of the tables at the şedinţe, those interminable brainwashing sessions that the Communist regime inflicted upon us and which were also held at tables covered in red cloths. I had never imagined to what extent a colour could cause one to switch from attraction to repulsion through the effect of subtle psychological mechanisms.

All this happened more than a quarter of a century ago but the images still remain vivid in my memory. After long hesitation, I eventually decided never to return to my own country. At the time, this attitude was called 'choosing freedom' and when close friends made me their honoured guest at the dinner-parties that appeared to me to be so incredibly lavish, I was always introduced as 'the Romanian-artist-painter-who-has-chosen-freedom'.

Unfortunately, I already wondered to what extent freedom could be relative, and oh how precarious it was! But, all in all, in the first place, what I sought was really this – to satisfy a visceral need to speak out, to read, to travel, a need that had been frustrated in me since childhood.

I also craved the freedom to meet people who were different, who thought differently, to freely converse with those who belonged to a 'different culture', to tell them about our own world, the one they lumped together as 'the Eastern bloc'. To deny or confirm the rumours, the information that had filtered through to them – Budapest/Bucharest, it was all the same to them – and to confront myself with a different environment, to leave me overawed by its richness and brilliance, to subsequently take the time to discover its limitations, contradictions and the features that it shared.

In this world that was becoming my own, I tried henceforward to adapt, to integrate, but I could never have succeeded in doing so without you, all of you, who had the patience to initiate me into the codes and values of this world that so intrigued me, whose brilliance exploded in my face.

*

During these naïve beginnings everything astonished me – the down-and-outs, the metro, the taxis, bank accounts, supermarkets and even the people who held down miserable, mundane little jobs and who seemed to have stepped out of a Pinter play; tantalised by this world that was new to me and that had been forbidden to me for so long, everything seemed to me to be imbued with an air of freedom. Since then, I have had the opportunity of becoming more lucid and I have gradually learned to step back from it and view it more dispassionately.

In any case, even during the first months, as if it were an alarm signal, I started to miss the afternoon siesta. Once the intoxication had passed, I began to experience a reaction from the initial exaltation.

Consequently, one day, I was suddenly afflicted by *dor*, a longing for a world that was no longer mine; the pain of being uprooted, that unforgiving pain, gripped my entrails.

To my great surprise, what paradoxically helped me to overcome the crisis which, I was told, afflicts every exile and every rootless soul, were the earthly foods, experienced through the warp of memory. An instinct immediately awakened in my veins, ordering me to delve into this memory of the senses, that which is linked to the foods of my homeland.

When I lived in Romania, I had been unfamiliar with the secrets of the art known as culinary – I couldn't even boil an egg – yet in the land of my exile I felt a vital need to reconstitute, then and there, the irreplaceable world of flavours and fragrances of my origins with which I had been impregnated since earliest childhood. So, resorting to pots and pans, I took my first steps as a novice, launching myself unremittingly into the cuisine of my country for which I felt nostalgia as intense as pain. I thus served an apprenticeship in the culinary arts as an initiation, through the specialised field of Romanian cuisine.

I began by writing to my mother, begging her to send me the recipes of which she alone knew the secret, those dishes which were part of the customs of the daily life of our family. I was convinced that this was how I was going to be able to reconstitute and relive the exact flavours of my childhood that I needed so badly in order to cure my sickness.

A mother understands. I soon received, wrapped in a crumpled Turkish rug of the type with which my mother used to adorn the walls of our flat in Bucharest, reminding me so vividly of its smells and its atmosphere, along with a few badly printed little books, an exercise book. This object was filled with a mother's love, of the *dor* she also felt in relation to me, in which she had carefully written down by hand her own recipes that might remind me of family moments in the past, and indeed all of them brought me the pleasure and comfort that I had hoped for. At the time, these objects were my crutches, a breath of fresh air, the salt and sugar that helped me to survive, to assuage my bitterness, to enable me to endure that difficult phase of rootlessness; without experiencing too many hard knocks, to gradually embrace a new life that continued to be mysterious, even as it was opening up in front of me. This initiation into Romanian culinary art also helped me to recover my mental health, as I improvised in Paris, in the precarious surroundings of my beginnings here, a corner of the Romania from which I found myself, as it were, amputated.

At the very beginning, in this maid's room – at least it was in the fashionable sixteenth arrondissement! – where I first found lodgings, I produced my earliest culinary offerings on a portable 'camping gas' stove, creating the sort of improvised Romanian meals that you will eventually be tasting, though I was rather nervous at first. And you also know that, one after the other, like a series of revelations, you experienced the strong flavours of the foods which you found as exciting as they were mysterious: bean purée, stuffed peppers, *borş* in all its variations, *chiftele*, several of the many variations of *plăcintă* and even the succulent *sarmale* that are so time-consuming to make. And finally, there was the *mămăligă*, the cornmeal polenta that is the central feature of Romanian cuisine which, not without a certain amount of pride, I ingeniously prepared for you and subsequently for the other guests who successively graced my table.

I very soon understood that, despite their distance, I had not lost these roots. Paradoxically, they grew miraculously within me, they inhabited me. They were impregnated with the culinary traditions of my country, and even more so with those of my family, or to even more distant origins, dating back perhaps to my Dacian ancestors? My heart and entrails were warmed with the wonderful fragrance of *borş*, my *sarmale* were redolent of dill and rosemary.

This desire to revive the flavours and odours that went right back to my childhood was not limited to the pure and simple tasting of a menu or the table of contents of any cookery book because, at the same time, it gave me an incentive to transmit a whole way of being, an atmosphere, a special environment from which, I believed, this culinary culture could not be dissociated.

Far from merely serving my own satisfaction, this joyous therapy that I had discovered for myself only became effective if I simultaneously communicated to my circle of friends the customs, tastes and smells that I myself perceived more sharply at the time, due to their painful absence. As soon as I had acquired the technical rudiments of this cuisine, I felt an intense need to transmit it to others, to revive it and recreate it in a new context, here, far from my homeland. This vision, conceived out of the typically Romanian joy and generosity which I so gladly inherited, fitted me like a glove.

Reverie over a certain Oyster Mushroom Stew
Third letter to Agnes

To calm me down, to provide relief from those violent bursts of melancholy that sometimes attacked me, I had a secret. All I had to do to cure myself was to peel an onion, and to do so slowly, at a leisurely pace, without hurrying. Then, heavy tears, those false tears that look so much like the real thing, would begin to flow, beneficent, liberating, generously bathing my cheeks, and I would be instantly filled with a sort of plenitude as if I were indulging in a pleasure.

I am standing in my kitchen and concentrating on skinning an onion. Peeling an onion. This primordial operation is, as everyone knows, the universal prelude to any serious cookery, indispensable to the creation of that universal main course of every country, which the French call *ragoût*, the English and Irish 'stew' and the Romanians *tocană*.

Today, I have guests coming. Romanian friends. I am improvising as I usually do, I embark on flights of fancy, letting myself be carried away by a chance but fortunate invention, a multicoloured stream of aromas, of random thoughts, exasperated by a fleeting odour that reaches me through the open window, or by a captivating splash of colour that held my gaze this morning as I strolled through the market in the rue de Lévis.

Sometimes, when I am cooking, I find myself abruptly seized by an insane desire to paint. In any case, I would compare cookery to art and love. They are all in the same vein, we experience similar emotions when coming into contact with them, whether we are

15

creating or tasting food. I sometimes surprise myself by applying the very same vocabulary of painting to that of cookery and to a certain way of tasting food.

Bizarrely, when standing in front of a sublime painting – I remember that it was a portrait of the great Romanian painter, *Tonița* – I started to salivate as I might have done when contemplating with anticipation a succulent dish or a delicious dessert. The same voluptuousness, the same interior joy spread through my body upon approaching this beauty as one experiences when one wants to eat.

At other times, the same type of feeling, normally linked to an appetite for food, would stimulate my salivary glands, attacking me with a sort of gluttony in the midst of a painting session, while I was mixing colours with a palette knife. The smooth, thick, shiny impasto and the pleasure of spreading it over the medium, the subtlety of a glaze, almost gave me a desire to swallow the material, squeezing tubes of cadmium yellow or cobalt blue all over the place; and each time this happened, I smiled internally because I found this strange tendency, this secret mischievousness, to be irresistibly amusing.

More deliberately, I would also play a game with myself, comparing the consistency or composition of a main dish or light starter, sometimes with the grace of a spontaneous sketch using lively, fleeting strokes, sometimes, in the case of a more carefully prepared, nourishing dish that had simmered on the stove for longer, to an elaborate, structured composition with powerful rhythms. I also amused myself by imagining a family relationship between a particular dish and the work of a famous painter. Thus, stews, hors d'oeuvres, charlottes and soufflés each received this dignifying association which, depending upon my inspiration, might be a Cézanne, a Degas, a Monet or even a Matisse. These great masters would probably not have been shocked to find their names among the pots and pans because, as is now known, a good many of them were happy to exchange their brushes for kitchen utensils and they cooked like artists.

As for me, I feel cookery through my fingertips and, just like the painting with which I am familiar, it is passionate, sensual, made from a flurry of rapid, feverish gestures, large brushstrokes applied voluptuously, leaving room here and there for calm, serene, tranquil expanses, the results of reverie and meditation. My own cookery style is closer to the gestures and freedom of style of a Delacroix, a Turner, a de Kooning or a Pollock, a long way, I admit, from the severe geometry of a Cézanne or a Mondrian, which in no way overshadows the admiration I feel for them. The way I have of launching myself into a whirlwind of action is no doubt the result of certain of my character traits, but it is also exacerbated by the constraints imposed by a life lived at a dizzying pace. Having embarked upon it without the right of appeal, I feel myself thrust onward by a desire that dashes ahead of me. I am tossed and turned in the course of rough days, alone in a modern city, I feel sick with longing for the time of my serene liberty, deprived of the fine time of my childhood, the time that is slipping through my fingers and is escaping from me, leaving me thirsting for it every day. And yet, miraculously, I sometimes rediscover a little of those shimmering, lost pieces of it at which I marvel. Especially when I cook. I cannot do without them, whatever the cost.

*

The queen-of-the-night seeds that a friend brought me from Romania have finally germinated. They are precious to me because these typically Romanian flowers cannot be found in France. I had recently planted them in the pot of earth that stands here in the kitchen close to my elbow, beside the shelves that serve as my work surface and that are covered by a multitude of little pots and bottles that provide me, at any given moment, with all the spices of the earth.

Finally, a few thin sprigs of a hesitant green have pierced the damp earth. When will they grow to the height of those Romanian flowers whose little star-shaped corollas, perched on long, leafy stems, perfumed the summer nights in grandfather's garden in *Râmnicu-Sărat?* We spent some of our holidays in that small provincial town in which my parents were born. Late at night, when a cooling breeze wafted up, a perfume that was both mellow and powerful filled the long summer evenings and seemed to us to slowly rise in the transparent air, up to the starry sky, along with the song of the crickets. It is for their habit of only coming to life at night that these mysterious flowers are called queen-of-the-night, because it is only in the dark that they consent to blossom, opening wide their petals to exude a delicious perfume as if in liberation. During the day, they are sad, hanging down their heads, flat and odourless, melting unremarked into the background.

*

This morning, there was a glut of wild mushrooms of every kind in the market. I wanted to bring home whole basketsful, they were so amazing in the diversity of their textures, the subtlety of their colours, the strangeness of their shapes, the variety of eccentric caps.

So for dinner tonight, why not a wild mushroom ragout, I said to myself. Who could resist the attraction of such a flavour? I could simmer them with a little meat into one of those Romanian stews, the hearty, thick, heavily spiced peasant dishes known in Romanian as *tocană* or *tochitură*. These are simple, substantial dishes with a virile, hearty flavour, 'manly' food consumed among friends in the low taverns in which men were wont to gather, since their atmosphere reminds them of the spiciness and freedom of the time in their lives when they were *burlac*, the Romanian word for 'bachelor'. And all of a sudden, I am reminded of my father, because I always imagined that he would have led that sort of life before his marriage, relatively late in life, to my mother. He often dreamed of it, I am sure, as of a paradise lost, because my mother restrained him with a firm but gentle hand, keeping him away from this sort of food which she considered to be vulgar and lacking in class.

With the feverishness of passion, compressed by time that flies by at speed, I accumulate the gestures that will culminate in this creation and I can already imagine it with its heady aroma, and all the colours to rejoice the eye, its wonderful odours, this work of art which could perhaps be – I am still hesitating – the *tocană* of the Hajduks or perhaps, invaded by a profusion of all sorts of vegetables, the lush *ghiveci*. I finally opt for a *tocană*. That is what I shall create for them. I say 'create' because my culinary feats often take on the aspect of events in the style of a happening – you know how fond I am of the playfulness of this spontaneous cuisine which I am constantly reinventing with an almost child-like joy.

Well, I feel that I am going to offer them, my friends, one of those larger-than-life Romanian meals. I'm sure it will be a *tocană*, made from pork and a mass of wild mushrooms. You will enjoy the recipe, I'm sure. I'll save it for you, like a snapshot capturing the moment, a few gestures to remind you of what it's like 'in the heat of battle'.

Tocană in my own style

As the basic ingredients, I take a mixture of pork ribs and loin which I cut into large pieces. I begin by frying them in a casserole and I am already impregnated with the delicious fumes that rise from them. The pieces of meat are then removed and kept warm separately. The fat is too indigestible so I discard it.

In the same pan, still redolent of the flavour of the meat, I fry a mass of onion rings, those that I talked about earlier when I have moments of intense meditation while peeling and slicing them. I add a few carrots sliced into rings – I appreciate the splash of colour, it's necessary; then I add anything I can find to give the dish more flavour – a piece of chilli pepper, a stick of celery, a few sprigs of herbs, dill, parsley, and so on.

Finally, I return the pieces of meat to the pan, I stir them, sprinkling them with a few pinches of flour which I incorporate by mixing with the inevitable wooden spoon. Finally, I sprinkle the contents of my casserole with two or three glasses of dry white wine – I always keep a half-bottle chilled – and then a litre and a half of stock. I lovingly cover the casserole, I keep watch over it and let it simmer for a good half hour, peeping inside from time to time to ensure that nothing is burning or sticking. Only towards the end of the cooking time, do I add salt and pepper with a firm gesture. Finally, I drop into the pot several coarsely chopped garlic cloves. Calmly, I let it simmer for another five to ten minutes. I inhale this good, rich fragrance, I feel myself imbued with it already.

Separately, in a different pot, I cook the wild mushrooms, which consist predominantly of oyster mushrooms. The result is an exciting, delicious mixture which is already producing the most appetising aromas. To cook them, I sprinkle them with one or two tablespoons of oil because I have to tell you that, in principle, butter is rarely used in Romanian cooking, and frankly, certainly not in the rustic tradition. I incorporate the mushrooms while they are still piping hot, combining them with the meat just before serving them at table and not forgetting to add three large tablespoons of cream to the sauce to make it more velvety. Of course, I don't forget to sprinkle the contents of the pot abundantly with chopped flat-leaved parsley and chopped dill which will produce the necessary tonic splash of bright green. A thick, firm, hot *mămăligă* is an essential accompaniment to the strong flavour of this dish which, I confess, is a mixture of known recipes, tinged with my own creativity. But it is truly Romanian in spirit. I can already see the smiling faces of my guests who have just taken a mouthful and I am exultant in anticipation.

As I pour strong red wine into their glasses, I imagine one of those 'full-bodied' Romanian wines, such as *Murfatlar*, or perhaps a few splashes of a good *ţuică* served in tiny glasses, I know that I have a little left in the bottle of this exquisite beverage that comes straight from the *Sibiu* region, it was packed in whatever came to hand when it was sent. The anonymous bottle, devoid of a label, is the indubitable proof of its origins, a healthy, genuine product of the Romanian *terroir*. There is no question, this comes straight from the producer, it hasn't been 'smuggled'. That is how, as you know, these pungent flavours give the best of themselves and find themselves exalted beyond all expression.

To complete this orchestration that is already close to the limits of perfection, I know that something piquant is lacking, those cucumbers pickled in brine that every Romanian loves. A pot kept in a cool place will no doubt be placed on the table before anything else. Or perhaps other pickled vegetables will be there to stimulate the appetite, such as the *gogonele*, green tomatoes pickled in brine, which delight Romanian gourmets who are such avid seekers of authenticity.

While my dish is simmering, even before the operation is complete, I give in to the desire to have a little 'snack', so I delve into the pot in which the oyster mushrooms from the rue de Lévis are singing. They aren't quite done, they have barely absorbed the flavour of the meat and the cooking liquid impregnated with a profusion of herbs and onions. That is how I love them. Imagine, they have already taken on a coppery tint and yet remain slightly crunchy. These tests do little to conceal, I admit, the most egotistic of eating pleasures but, for every cook, they have the advantage of offering the most exquisite moments and will remain his or her true reward, while awaiting the presumed plaudits of the diners. A few mouthfuls stolen on the fly, munched almost on one's lap, are far more delicious than the finished dish, as it will eventually be placed on the table, under the trembling eyes and nostrils of the famished guests who will throw themselves upon it, blissfully unaware of all the preludes that only its creator will have accomplished with fervour in the secrecy of her kitchen. That is why one often sees very little of her, because she is already satisfied and at table she merely presents a mysteriously fulfilled face and an absence of hunger that the others find suspicious.

*

So, there you are, I am confiding in you these last few gestures, they are also part of what I would call 'the culinary event'. I help myself to a serving of three large tablespoons of oyster mushroom stew which I transfer to a small dish. I season it abundantly with salt and pepper, I sprinkle it with a few crushed garlic cloves, a little chopped flat-leaved parsley and dill and I incorporate a good tablespoon of cream just as I will do for the real dish when it is ready and when the finishing touches have been added. With half-closed eyes, I taste, dumbstruck with admiration, these few mouthfuls along with

21

a piece of wholemeal bread and, to better accompany the flavours that have just emerged from under my fingers, I serve myself a small glass of claret, sipping it in small mouthfuls. Once the real dish is finished, I won't feel like tasting it. I tell myself that this improvisation perfectly offers me the essentials of the real 'Romanian flavour'. It is impossible to describe, a question of proportions, an appreciation that only a Romanian could understand, only a Romanian could tell me that I am right.

Esti

Fourth letter to Agnes

I have often mentioned, dear Agnes, 'the big-hearted maid' who was so close to us. How could I forget her? Esti. It sometimes seems to me that she is still here, somewhere, watching what I do in the kitchen. I often think about her, her plump figure, the mischievous grin that wreathed her round, white face that was as pale as the moon.

From the depths of Transylvania, where she was born on an uncertain date that must have been just before the end of nineteenth century, in a little village called *Iedu*, which means 'kid' in Romanian, Esti came to us one day shortly before Christmas. She had left home after having been disappointed in love, a secret that she hid from us for many years, and came to Bucharest to visit a friend who happened to be the concierge of our building, in the hope of forgetting her heartache. My mother, who was pregnant with me, was looking for a cook; taken on trial, Esti was not to leave us until she died. She was to become, no one doubted it from the beginning, the central character of our domestic life, the apex of the pyramid, the person who watched over the destiny of our family food; and far more, that of the 'cookery of the soul'. She deserved this place of honour in the highest degree through the devotion and love that she showed us unreservedly for four decades.

From the start, her optimism in the face of every trial and tribulation, buoyed up by an enormous vitality and, of course, her extraordinary skills as a cook, enabled her to conquer everyone. Her gaiety was contagious and, like her violent but short-lived fits of temper, everything she did was in the superlative. The good nature and good health that she radiated were such that one merely had to encourage her to laugh for her to be unable to stop.

*

Oh those fits of laughter, so tonic and droll, they still resound in my head. Those bursts of mirth, vigorous, invasive, she was possessed by them; when that happened, the curves of her body were shaken to their smallest fibre and the spectacle itself became so comical that we were dragged into laughing with her, the laughter of the good child that is so catching in its spontaneity.

Whether kneading dough, ironing the linen, washing the floor tiles or stirring the *mămăligă*, all these gave her an opportunity to move her robust being in a sort of frenzied joy that she radiated around her; her face would turn pink, drops of fine perspiration covered her forehead and it seemed as though no one could stop her drive. She devoted herself wholeheartedly to the task and it was from this life of intense activity that she drew her energy, vitality and joy. I think she was a genuinely happy person.

Esti was completely illiterate. She had not been altered or changed by any culture, leaving her original candour intact and pure. She had always been there, as far as I was concerned. I only remember her as an old woman and I have an unchanging image of her over the years. She must have been close to forty when she became part of our family and I left Romania about ten years before her death.

She was short, well-built, sturdy, almost round without actually being fat, and her body had a warm fragrance, with something animal about it, which combined with the smells of the kitchen where she spent most of her time. Her delicate white skin had a baby's softness and transparency. I think her hair must have turned white very early in life because I never saw her looking otherwise. She did not tint it or cut it, but wore it in a tight bun held in place with enormous metal pins on her short, thick neck. In the rare moments when she let it loose to comb it out with smooth strokes, it fell right to the ground and we contemplated it in amazement. To perform this ritual, before nightfall, she would sit by the window at the same kitchen table that she had cleared of all utensils. In these instances of grace, bathed in the evening light, she became an unreal figure, a priestess officiating at some pagan rite.

Esti had her own way of dressing, with a certain coquettishness, and she never wore just any old thing. She always wore dresses with a deeply plunging neckline and short sleeves that showed off her short, strong arms and the beginnings of her generous bust. Esti hated long sleeves, she told us that they restricted her movements. If she was given a long-sleeved dress as a gift, even if it were made of silk, she would soon get to work on it with a few barbarous cuts of the scissors; she would then appear, wreathed in smiles, ingenuously revealing her arms that were naked to the shoulder.

Yet there was nothing shocking about her clothing which might have looked licentious or even ridiculous on a woman of her age and build, because she did it with such innocence and in such an amusing way that her mode of dress was accepted as part of her personality.

Esti was endowed with excessive sentimentality and extreme sensitivity. On our birthdays, she would use her cracked hands, their fingers reddened with hard work, to create wreaths of flowers, peonies, marguerites and dahlias and she would perch on a chair to nail them herself around the door of our children's bedroom. In order to prepare us for this delightful surprise that she had made into a spontaneous tradition, she would rise at dawn to be able to watch us passing under this flowery triumphal arch. She would thus make us happy as sandboys and the echo of our happiness was reflected in her as if in a mirror, as at these moments her face shone and blossomed like a perfectly open cabbage.

Each time we went away on holiday, even if it was only for a few days, she would weep hot tears that she would wipe away with the back of her hand or the corner of her apron. We would be devastated and rush to hug her but she would turn her head away in a gesture of modesty. Embarrassed at having thus displayed her emotions, she would quickly retreat to the kitchen moving with her self-assured waddle.

Like summer showers, her tears or far rarer fits of anger would not last long and her optimism would soon gain the upper hand. But she was also capable of being authoritarian or excessively obstinate. When she got something into her head, no one could make her change her mind. Thus, all our efforts to make her eat at table with us, even though she meant more to us than our own grandmother, were in vain. She insisted on maintaining the customs of times past. Faithful to an archaic formality, she always insisted on addressing us in the third person, and hardly ever by our first names, but using 'titles' that she pronounced in her strong Transylvanian accent, with its staccato style and very open vowels which is untranslatable for you. I was *Domnişora* (a sort of 'Miss'), my little brother was the only exception in the family, graced with the far less formal title of *Puiu*, which means 'chicken', a nickname that accompanied him right up until military service. My mother was addressed as *Coniţa* and my father was *Conaşu'*, old-fashioned forms of address equivalent to 'Sir' or 'Madam', a fossilised trace of the era in which servants showed their lords and masters a devotion and respect that did not exclude a deep affection and even a certain dominating familiarity. We liked to compare Esti with Scarlett O'Hara's mammy in *Gone with the Wind* because we could easily imagine her in that role, surrounded by that aura of romanticism and naïvety. Like a mammy, Esti fussed over us with that mixture of authority and extreme intimacy, and the way that 'Missie Scarlett's mammy addressed her was easily comp-rable to the *Domnişoara* Sanda that Esti used when talking to me.

She also told us that back there, in Transylvania, she had worked, since the age of fifteen, in the great families of the *boieri* (boyars) or for the Hungarian *grofi* (counts). That is where she must have acquired the ingrained habits to which she clung come what may, preserving them with a pride that had something quixotic about it.

For instance, right to the end, she used to use such little expressions as: 'Would *Domnişoara* please take her breakfast...' or 'Could *Coniţa* come and see this...' 'Would *Conaşu'* come and drink his soup...'. This did not prevent her from upsetting the family atmosphere on

26

occasion with the slightly dictatorial airs she permitted herself to assume due to her long presence in our family.

But above all, it was through the various practices of cookery that Esti expressed the whole dimension of her personality. She would comply with each of our caprices, our sudden cravings or desires for impromptu dinners, tackling them with the same brio as the elaborate feasts she prepared for important occasions; she was always able to handle the complexity of these multiple lunches during the day, resulting from our various timetables, complying with our slightest eccentricities. Nothing would spoil her willingness and eagerness for work. Pleasing everyone remained her highest aspiration, giving was the very purpose of her existence.

I can see her again in the narrow kitchen, enveloped in the fragrant odours that escaped from her steaming saucepans. She usually stood over a cooking-pot, armed with a wooden spoon that she would dip into the gently simmering mass of a fragrant stew, tasting it from time to time and always noisily smacking her lips.

Curiously, we didn't often see her eating and we used to say that she would feed her plump body through her pores, so impregnated were they throughout the day with the substantial emanations of her cooking. In fact, we understood that these frequent tastings were amply sufficient for her nourishment and in some way came to replace the regular meals that she had quite naturally eliminated perhaps unconsciously.

The crude wooden table beside the window which was her work surface had become impregnated over the years with the cooking medium, a rich patina and the multiple traces of the scars imprinted on it by the daily activities linked to cookery. It was on this rudimentary cutting-board that had been in use for so long, that Esti prepared a fair number of the special dishes whose secrets were known only to her. It is here that with expert hands she rolled out the dough to an extraordinary thinness to make a *plăcintă*, a delicious flaky pastry pie. It is here also that she vigorously kneaded the dough for *cozonac*, before the Christmas and Easter holidays, chopping into minute pieces with the consummate art of a goldsmith, onion, garlic and herbs for stews and *chifetele* (meatballs). Again, it was at this table that she officiated with authority, almost always standing, to fill fresh ravioli with spinach or cheese or turning the handle on some primitive item of kitchen equipment to make sausages or *caltaboş* for Christmas.

Certain more delicate and energy-sapping operations eventually forced her to sit in a chair. This was when she put on her glasses, their round lenses held in place in a thin metallic frame, and they would drop down to the end of her nose, giving her a faintly comical air. At these moments, concentrating intensely, she would prepare herself for a *sarmale*-making session, creating the stuffed cabbage leaves that are our true national dish. We would contemplate her with affectionate amusement while she dug her chubby fingers into a large basin to extract little pieces of the fragrant filling, carefully wrapping it in cabbage leaves made soft and flexible through having been pickled in brine.

As she shaped each *sarmale*, she would arrange it in a large, welcoming cooking pot. The cabbage rolls had to be tightly packed together so that they would become impregnated with the cooking liquid, the little pieces of smoked bacon and the white wine that Esti generously poured all over them. From time to time, she would count them, pointing at them with her little finger, the one that had become slightly twisted due to gout. At the end of this complex labour, she would proudly proclaim the result of the balance sheet of this gourmet account, satisfied once again to have beaten her previous record, 'I have made fifty-seven!' or 'ninety!' she was heard to exclaim. Her knowledge of arithmetic was limited to this operation, to the counting of her *sarmale* with her little finger.

Then she would carefully lift the heavy pot, filled with such riches, and immediately slide it into the oven where it would be left to simmer gently for several hours of true odoriferous ecstasy for the effluvia it emitted were truly irresistible. This was not an everyday dish because *sarmale* are a speciality, a culinary feat reserved for great occasions, and especially for the Christmas holidays.

Just before the end of the cooking time, Esti would remove the lid of the pot to allow the sauce in which the *sarmale* were cooked to reduce and for them to develop a pleasant golden crust on the surface. The *sarmale* were served with a hot *mămăligă* and a pot of sour cream with which they could be lavishly doused.

That was Esti. For a long time, she seemed to be the very incarnation of perfection. It was only later we discovered what could be described as her 'dark side'. These were not really faults, just adorable little peccadilloes, naughtinesses. We accepted these revelations with a smile of malicious satisfaction; in the end, not even Esti was blameless! And seeing her in this new light, endeared her to us all the more.

In fact, we were all too well aware of one of the 'vices' that Esti practised openly – that of gambling. Esti gambled, as she did everything else, with a dedicated and disinterested passion. This passion was so total that the pleasure of gambling far outweighed the satisfaction of winning. Yes, Esti played the lottery.

And what was so surprising is that she hardly ever won. Yet, nothing daunted, she would do it again each time spending the few pennies she had been able to save.

It may not have been a coincidence that she had become obsessed with this craze, at the very period when she began obstinately to refuse to leave the flat. As mysteriously as it was unexpected, one fine day, she confided in us that she would no longer be going down into the street. Never. It was as if she had entered a convent. Determined as she was, she remained faithful to this decision right to the end, though with a few minor exceptions which she eventually managed to do without. She would stride through the flat from one end to the other, making the wooden flooring creak, when the rare moment came for her to break her vow and go out. She would only do so as a result of our exhortations, and when she did so she would take stumbling, hesitant steps like those of a drunkard. Confused by her disorientation, she refused to do it again. This strange symptom was analysed by my mother, who described it as agoraphobia, one of those learned terms which seemed to us to be too pompous, especially in connection with Esti, and which is the medical term for 'panic-stricken fear of open spaces'. The roots of this problem were unknown to us, and we gradually became accustomed to this quirk of Esti's.

From this moment on, Esti organised herself, surrounding herself with external support. As for her 'gaming', she delegated the concierge or cleaning woman for the common parts of the building to buy her lottery tickets for her; later, my brother inherited this mission. His role also consisted in looking at the results in the newspaper and, an even more delicate task, to give her the news, which was usually bad. Once a week, my brother would take every precaution to ensure that the shock was not too painful, especially as Esti had spent part of the week building up her wildest dreams about 'what she would do with the money she had won'. In general, she would have distributed it generously to right and left, but to us, the members of 'her' family, as a priority.

Her dreams included the wildest fantasies which she insisted in formulating, even before she had found out the result. Sumptuous banquets headed the list, but there were also houses, cars (there existed not the trace of a private car in Romania at the time) and all sorts of gifts designed to make all our most extravagant dreams come true in one go. Esti accepted the news of these repeated disappointments with an exemplary dignity, with just a little giggle of self-derision followed by the same reply issued from an admirable wisdom which to some extent became our family motto: '*No*, if I haven't won, someone else must have done so...'. This '**no**', pronounced 'noh' was a Transylvanianism which had remained embedded like a sort of ancient relic in her vocabulary.

As for the other sin, one practised more discreetly, and that is why we were unaware of it for so long, it is something that we Romanians call with compassion and tender understanding for those who are affected by it 'the gift of drink'. Yes, Esti was, in fact, possessed by this 'gift'. In other words, she was a secret drinker. Nor did she drink just anything, no, it was 'the hard stuff', strong spirits, ţuică, a plum brandy that can be up to sixty per cent proof.

I don't remember how or at what moment her secret was discovered. The fact is that she hid under her mattress the 'little bottle' that she got Tinca to buy for her. Tinca was a well-built woman, a sort of colossus, who at the time lived on the fifth floor, in one of the maids' rooms. She was known as 'the Golem'.

There was a long-standing complicity between the two women. Esti was committed to a firm friendship, mixed with a respectful admiration for this former maid who had become a factory worker when her former masters emigrated to Israel. For her part, Tinca looked upon Esti in a spirit of protection and affection from the top of her monumental frame. This type of attitude was no doubt part of her destiny because she provided the proof equally in respect of her husband, a person who often featured in Esti's reports under the name of *Domnu' Ionel* ('Mr. Ionel'). I never met him but he was spoken of as a frail and suffering creature who, in fact, soon died, despite the devoted care lavished upon him by Tinca.

'It was a beautiful death' Esti told us after the burial, 'One could see that *Cocona Tinca* had looked after him well'.

Cocona was another way of saying 'Madam' although not quite as honourific and formal as *Coniţa* which was used for my mother – always pronounced in Esti's Transylvanian accent.

Tinca was one of those characters who were brought close to our family through being a neighbour and our friendship strengthened over the years. My mother, 'Madam the doctor' as she was sometimes called, was happy to offer medical advice and care, as she did for so many others. But Tinca also found herself, in exchange for a sort of tip, being associated with domestic tasks, especially if they required a certain amount of physical effort. For example, about twice a year, she helped Esti to beat the carpets. There were a lot of them in our house. In a spring-cleaning session that had Esti dashing about like a madwoman, the carpets were dragged down the back stairs and into the little interior courtyard. After throwing the carpet over a strong rope stretched between two walls, she would start to beat them firmly with a large, rigid wicker carpet-beater. Esti often welcomed her great friend into the kitchen from the back stairs and they could be found chatting, discussing the rain and the fine weather, in a cloud of the cheap tobacco from the cigarettes which Tinca, a heavy smoker, would smoke to the very tip of the butt.

A Letter from Italy

Fifth letter to Agnes

> *'...We need to become re-accustomed to the pleasure*
> *that the contemplation of the outside world*
> *procures which is magnificent...'*
> David Hockney

I am writing to you from Florence. Yes, *Firenze*, its real name, if you prefer it. It is the height of the season, the city is drowning in a cohort of tourists, yet I always manage to find myself a few expanses of beneficial solitude, of self-reliance, enabling me to fully appreciate this necessary change of scenery. For two hours, I have been wandering aimlessly, lingering in the alleyways and on the bridges of Florence, keeping as far away as possible from the tourist hotspots. During these wanderings, I have let myself be overwhelmed by its indescribable beauty, my eyes caress the ancient patina of its walls.

Seated at a table in a little *trattoria*, still rain-soaked from a sudden shower, I wait for the *zuppa di verdura* that I have ordered in my broken Italian. I have little difficulty in detecting, at nearby tables, those anonymous faces wreathed in beatific, credulous smiles, disarming in their innocence, that I call 'the tourist smile'. But to tell the truth, am I not also a tourist? Am I not myself someone who has also come from elsewhere and who is constantly searching for those details, that 'authenticity' that so often is a mere series of clichés, with as little perception and the same childish and ridiculous hyperbolic enthusiasm?

Come on, let's try and put ourselves on the other side of the barrier and distance ourselves from these inanities; it is not in these tawdry, commercial places that one will taste the authentic cuisine of a country, its true spirit.

The *zuppa di verdura*, *osso bucco* and various types of pasta that the owner serves me will never equal the simple quality of the unpretentious dishes that I simmer on the stove as a 'mum' like the woman spying on us at this very moment from the house opposite, hiding in the shadow behind the curtain that she is twitching. Yes, I am convinced that each culinary culture gives of its best in the form that I would call 'mother's cooking', the only one that is authentic and inimitable.

*

Taking a break like this always leads me into a reverie, and out of this comes a desire to write... So I am taking a piece of paper, the wait seems to be long, but I have all the time in the world. It's so good not to be in a hurry.

Installed comfortably with an opened *mezzo rosso*, I just need a moment of respite so that my thoughts can once again drag themselves back into the past, surrounding that mythical time of my life spent in Romania. Childhood, Esti, Mama, my father, my little brother; our dear little home in Bucharest, when we all lived there together.

Dear friend, I'd like you to imagine the atmosphere that flourished around the Romanian food about which I have so often talked to you and that I have given you to taste more than once. In a four-storey building in the very centre of Bucharest, this tiny flat – it couldn't have measured more than sixty square metres – was furnished with that slightly eccentric charm, that irreplaceable poetry resulting from a diverse selection of objects, furniture and carpets, a lot of carpets. They were all over the place, on walls, on the floor, draped over a shabby old armchair, those Turkish or Persian carpets accumulated by my mother, who was a passionate antique-hunter, completely self-taught. And yet, despite the imperfections and things that were lacking, there was nothing there that was dead, ugly or boring, and above all the vulgar pursuit of the new was absent.

Our flat consisted of what estate agents now call a 'double reception room' and two bedrooms that we shared in a sort of tender intimacy of which we were not even aware since it was more or less how most families lived on a daily basis, especially in Bucharest, due to the housing shortage that had become chronic. It was a place where one felt good, which all our friends loved to visit, its door was always open wide to guests and the few unusual details merely accentuated its poetry and charm, there was always a new magical item of interest.

Above all, I can see, I don't know why, the enigmatic presence of that little stuffed eagle, perched over the sideboard, whose outspread wings dominated the landscape of the dining room. The eagle was a vestige of the hunting parties on which my father used to go when he was still a bachelor so it probably dated from the 1930s. It frightened me at first, that eagle, but later I came to accept it, it had such a touching air, frozen in flight. And it eventually merged into the rest of the decor.

It was thus in the shadow of this little eagle from the 1930s that our meals took place, at that black lacquered 'cubist style' dining set that my parents, as a young couple who wanted to be 'modern', had bought with the rest of the furniture, just before the war, in 1935 to be precise.

With time, the dining-room furniture took on a dark brown moiré shade, for it was never replaced. It consisted of a square table that could be extended to accommodate twelve people thanks to its two leaves, and a dozen of square chairs upholstered in a fabric in several shades of beige, a display cabinet filled with all sorts of china and a miscellaneous collection of trinkets of doubtful worth but not without their charm and finally, in the same lacquered black style, the long sideboard on which there sat a not insignificant item, the wooden radio set manufactured by Telefunken. This large, very long sideboard contained the tableware, everyday china, my mother's lovely damask table napkins, a few *petit fours* or biscuits, as well as the most secret part that was locked up, in which were stored numerous jars of jam and preserves, the temptation of the forbidden.

The radio set was a real object of desire, destined to capture, very laboriously in fact due to the sound being jammed by a permanent screen of complex noise, the programmes broadcast by the free radio stations in the West, such as Radio Free Europe, the Voice of America and the BBC. These were a valuable and unique source of information destined to fill the massive gaps of which we had been the regular victims for decades. These 'tuning in' sessions, of which my father was exclusively in charge, were generally held after nine o'clock, which was when we ate our evening meal, and they became part of the family's nightly ritual. Television had not yet made its appearance in the homes of the period and local radio programmes mostly broadcast nothing but propaganda, so these sessions were a sort of precarious and primitive substitute for entertainment. But they were far more than just 'something to do', they were beneficial as the only means of access to the outside world, as precious as a drop of water to a thirsty traveller lost in the desert. The broadcasts, through their probity, attractiveness and effectiveness, had acquired an indisputable authority which no one could be unaware of, even members of the *nomenclatură*, the Communist hierarchy, despite the fact that they were officially forbidden.

*

What were our mealtimes like? Were they governed by a monastic rigour or did a more permissive, liberal spirit prevail?

Well, I must confess that our meals had nothing austere about them, despite my mother's efforts to make a pretend attempt at severity. The atmosphere was spontaneous, even permissive – although in this we were an untypical family. I do not claim to present to you here, in everything I am telling you, a prototype of the behaviour shared by all Romanian families, I am writing about 'my' family, whom I consider to be an individual, actual case of a Romanian family.

At any event, our meals did not begin with a prayer, something I later saw in the cinema. Nor did they continue with rigorous sessions of collective mastication, heads lowered, without uttering a word, elbows pressed tightly against the body and with no one being allowed to move more than necessary for feeding, exchanging the minimum of words, only to ask for the salt to be passed, for example. No, this type of scene – which I am parodying of course – was nothing like what I experienced.

I can still hear the voice of poor Mama calling each of us to the table, in every tone of voice, starting mildly, then more forcefully, and finally shrieking with irritation and exasperation. She thus succeeded with difficulty in dragging us away from our various preoccupations. I was the worst culprit, with my habit of walking about barefoot and sitting at table cross-legged on my chair. This spontaneous behaviour earned me the semi-ironic, semi-complacent nickname of 'the family gypsy' that I retained for many years.

These insistent calls would continue for more than half an hour. They were always about dinner or the Sunday meals, and you will soon learn why. Finally, when her strenuous efforts had finally borne fruit, we were assembled around the table, lured in part by the wonderful smells emanating from the kitchen and pangs of ravenous hunger.

My little brother, Barbu – five years younger than me – had a habit of installing himself at the table with a book from which he was incapable of separating himself since he still had 'half a paragraph to finish'. After he arrived, there came my father, absorbed by radio broadcasts from the free world that he tried to capture through the thick curtain of noise which reminded us of the echoes of some sort of imminent cataclysm. Sometimes, he would be hunched up, armed with an extremely thin pair of tweezers, a sort of monocle screwed into his eye-socket, devoting himself to repairing an old Swiss watch, a sort of 'miniature-do-it-yourself' that he practised with a passion for the same meticulous care with which he did everything else. As for me, I was sometimes the one who straggled in last, because I was still trying to decipher a passage or two from a Beethoven sonata or a Chopin nocturne – the piano was a sort of artistic hobby for me – when I wasn't in a full painting session, confined to my improvised studio.

Family dinners were finally moments of relaxation and gaiety because, despite this rather uncertain start, once we were finally seated at table, we enjoyed to the full the wonderful dishes that Esti or my mother had cooked up for us, and we would discuss the thousands of things that had happened during the day...

A detail that may surprise you is the fact that Romanians were in the habit of dining at 9.30 in the evening or even later. This eccentricity was the result of a whole 'timetable culture' specific to Romanians who had adopted the continuous working day a long time ago, starting at six or seven o'clock in the morning and working until two or three in the afternoon. Then they would go home and not return to work until the following day. That is why meals were inserted into the day at times that were very different from those of France or England.

Here is the rhythm of these Romanian days. What the origin of this custom is, I have no idea. Perhaps it is due to the so-called continental climate, with its hot, dry summers. In the early afternoon the heat becomes suffocating, and this is when people shut themselves indoors in search of some shade, lowering the blinds and closing the shutters; then there are the harsh winters when a biting cold covers all the roads and pavements in a thick coating of black ice – the highways would often be blocked by snowdrifts. At that time of year, it was best to leave work early enough to be able to get home well before nightfall.

So my parents, like the mass of working people, left home at seven in the morning or even earlier and worked right through until the early afternoon or even mid-afternoon, when they would finally come home for lunch. Lunch was the well-deserved main meal of the day. It was hearty, nourishing and carefully prepared and we lingered at it unashamedly, in fact we cherished it.

This was the moment when Esti busied herself over the stove in order to be able to welcome my parents home 'as is befitting' with delicious little dishes that were adapted to each family member's taste. This was done after we, the children, had been fed as well as the other people who sometimes happened to be in the flat for one reason or another, an uncle or an aunt, a grandfather or a classmate. The result was almost a series of lunches consumed at intervals, something which never seemed to be a problem, thanks to the presence and total availability of Esti, our house-elf.

As for the late evening meals, they were a sort of reward for a long, continuous working day and an addition to the lavish lunch which always took some digesting. But before that, between the two meals, there was the siesta, that ancient custom, that blessed rest, so well deserved and restorative after an inadequate night's sleep, so welcome after too copious a meal. I did not know at the time to what extent I would miss a banal and insignificant detail such as the siesta when I came to live in France; it revealed itself as a crucial element of this change of direction, symbolic of my new way of life.

Between the siesta and dinner, after the Turkish coffee break, a few hours were dedicated to domestic chores and various pastimes. This is an outline of how a Romanian spends the day, a series of moments and activities that are part of everyone's daily routine, and nothing has changed since.

In our house, as well as the homes of most city-dwelling families, weekday dinners were held after what the Romanians call a 'light evening tea'. This habit may have been introduced due to the period of austerity because I do not think that previous generations practiced it, at least according to what my parents have told me.

I must specify, however, that this 'tea' had nothing British about it, despite its name. First of all, that was because we only knew one type of tea, *ceai rusesc* or Russian tea, with its minute, thin black leaves. Nor was it drunk in the afternoon with biscuits, like the English; it was only drunk in the morning at breakfast and then later in the evening when it was consumed with more substantial food, a little like an American brunch or what the English call high tea.

Mama was a devotee of tea. This is how it was drunk in our house. First we would make a very concentrated infusion which turned as black as ink and which we would keep for several days in a little silver-plated teapot decorated with a minute engraved design as graceful as it was bizarre. The substance thus obtained was known as *esenţa* 'essence'. Each time the tea would then be made by pouring a few drops of this concentrated brew into each cup – these were beautiful porcelain cups found by my mother on one of her antique hunts; the rest of the cup would then be filled with boiling water. Sugar was added, a slice of lemon, and sometimes a little rum that was kept in a small crystal jug, topped with a cut-glass stopper. This little pitcher which leaned to one side always reminded me of a sparrow. The two vessels which were indispensable for making 'tea the way we drink it at home' took on the importance of symbols that are naturally inscribed into a permanent way of life, among a host of other 'special objects' in our daily world. I still have these little objects, here they are in front of me, on a shelf; their presence is so dear to me, I could not bear to be parted from them.

You mean 'typically Romanian'?
(*mămăliga*, dill and the rest)
Sixth letter to Agnes

How should Romanian cuisine be defined? How can it be distinguished from the other culinary cultures that resemble it? What is most quintessential about it, its true identity? In what does its inimitable character lie?

There is no easy answer to such questions. Even Romanians themselves have difficulty in replying. As far as I am concerned I would find it less hard to describe my own family's cooking, which is the food I would use as an example... And I could go on talking about it forever. With all its surrounding atmosphere...

Romanians would offer a whole host of different answers, it is that which gives them their charm. They will always find a way of starting a discussion, ever ready to argue and split into little groups of opinions, merely in response to a simple question such as this about the essence of their own cuisine.

Does this not constitute another irrefutable proof of the great richness of this cuisine, which is a real melting-pot of the multiple influences generously combined throughout the eventful history of this little country? Is it not living proof of the creativity of the nation that has brought to life such a diversity of modes of expression, depending on the region and even the families in a particular town?

Only a few days ago, some of my fellow-countrymen were at my house and I was once again provided with the proof of my theory. I listened in to lively commentaries, the moment the conversation turned dangerously towards that crucial subject, the specific nature, so difficult to pinpoint, of Romanian cooking. We all proclaimed with one voice, loudly and strongly, our irritation with the frequency of such situations when we have to deal with French questioning on this subject. This is when the discussion was triggered with its habitual vivacity. You ought to have seen, my dear, how this little group of Romanians was suddenly reanimated with all the symptoms of typically Romanian individualism. In fact, the whole world knows to what extent Romanians are individualistic and how the spirit of contradiction that is meat and drink to them. It is said, in fact, that when you have two Romanians you have two political parties. Furthermore, my compatriots are extremely voluble, never short of topics of conversation, which is why discussion is a veritable Romanian national institution.

So this is briefly why a short, pithy phrase inserted at the beginning of a discourse can result in a sort of improvised colloquium that will last for hours, without any concrete conclusion ever being reached. And that is precisely one of the most typical traits of these gabfests, the fact that no conclusion is ever reached. Needless to say, when the discussions are abundantly fuelled with liquid refreshment, the result is an inflamed atmosphere and the verbal exchanges of words become even more highly charged than usual.

*

After offering an initial toast, someone will set the tone and express an opinion, perhaps a rather original one, by affirming that it is definitely the use of dill that is the essence of Romanian cooking. This herb, a member of the aniseed family, with its needle-like, dark green leaves is known in Romanian as *mărar* and is used to impart a pleasant flavour to salads and sauced dishes. It is now time for everyone else to protest vehemently. Some of the company, contributing typically Romanian erudition, reply that the Scandinavians also use this herb in their food, and it is even used by the Germans and the English, under the name of 'dill' I think. That is how the first proposition comes to be rejected.

42

Finally, another current of opinion arises and its defenders reply in chorus, 'But no, it definitely has to be the *sarmale*', that filling food which most Romanians consider to be their native dish par excellence, those pieces of pickled cabbage leaf filled with a stuffing that gives off the richest of aromas, especially during the Christmas holidays. These are the most symbolic heart of Romanian cooking. Another person mentions that, in fact, it is the ancient and primitive habit of munching a raw onion, and especially with a good *mămăligă*. I think it was this remark that triggered a massive chorus of approval, by association of ideas. At the end of the day, most opted for *mămăligă* as representing the very essence of authentic Romanian cooking. I declared myself to be a convinced supporter of that last current of opinion.

True, a rather timid voice emerged from somewhere suggesting that *mămăligă* was similar to the Italian polenta, but no one paid any attention. The die had been cast. At any event, the function of Italian polenta as part of a meal, its consistency, its relationship to other foods, was not the same as for *mămăligă*. And that is how this last contender was soon eliminated and *mămăligă* emerged as the unanimous winner.

As far as I am concerned, *mămăligă* is indeed the one – and when I speak of it, I feel my mouth filling with the taste of that food which remains synonymous with what might be called the 'typically Romanian flavour'. In fact, one cannot even speak of flavour but rather of lack of flavour, a pleasant blandness. Curiously, *mămăligă*, boiled cornmeal, does not really have a flavour. How strange, you will exclaim, to place as the peak of perfection in the cuisine of a country a dish that is so ordinary, so everyday! Well, let me continue. It is the sensation that it produces in the mouth which combines admirably with the other dishes or foods that it accompanies. Its role is secondary yet vital, the enhancement, the bringing out of other flavours, of stimulating and completing.

Yes, that bright, golden yellow substance brings life to our plates, served steaming hot or else cold, whether thick or much lighter, almost liquid, depending on taste and circumstance, in all its variations and uses. Romanians cannot do without it and a Romanian meal would not be worthy of the name without the reassuring presence of *mămăligă*.

It is of *mămăligă* that I think when I want to plunge back into that atmosphere of home. Esti or Mama would often make it for us, serving it with a large slice of *telemea*, a salty ewe's milk cheese that is compact without being hard and brilliantly white in colour. It hails from the same family as the Greek feta cheese but it is creamier and fattier. The cheese would be topped with a dollop of sour cream in the classic way, with a nice mound of *mămăligă* next to it. That is how we tackled it, and, best of all, accompanied by a raw onion that we would crunch between our teeth, a custom that some might describe as barbaric.

At other times, *mămăligă* would serve the role of attenuating the strong, pungent, bitingly sharp, peppery taste of stews such as the delicious *tocană*, or fish dishes such as carp *saramură*, in which the fish is grilled and then smothered in a garlicky brine, flavoured with herbs. *Mămăligă* is also in good company with the famous 'fishermen's *borş*' from the Danube delta, a Romanian bouillabaisse. It is a sour soup, a rich stew in which the heads of freshwater fish, especially carp, are used to make an exquisite broth which some people do not hesitate to enhance with a tiny green chilli pepper to set the mouth on fire. That is how the really macho Romanian men like it, those leathery-skinned individuals brought up the hard way, who boast of how they can crunch on the fieriest of whole chillies as a means of proving their virility.

In the country – although Mama continued this ancient tradition – there was a charming habit of using the contrast between cold and hot when the remains of a *mămăligă* from the night before would be steeped in very hot, slightly salted milk. Or then doing the reverse and pouring cold, even ice-cold, milk over a lump of boiling hot *mămăligă* cooked for so long that it was almost hard. In the country, this would have been eaten in the evening with the whole family sitting round a low table on wooden stools. The food would have been served in lovely enamelled earthenware bowls and eaten with wooden spoons. The feeling of contrast between the two substances, the earthenware and the wood, would give a feeling of well-being and a softness that married wonderfully with the consistency of the *mămăligă*. The result was a harmonious effect that went perfectly with 'the spirit of *mămăligă*'.

Mămăligă would be cooked for a long time in the huge cooking-pot, known as a *ceaun*, that would have become blackened with use. When cooled, the *mămăligă* would solidify and could easily be cut into thick slices with a string, as in the fishing villages where it was eaten instead of bread.

My father used to tell me stories that fired my imagination about how *mămăligă* and sheep's cheese, *telemea*, had always been the basic diet of the Romanian peasant. And when you say peasant, you mean a Romanian since until quite recently the peasant class accounted for eighty per cent of the population. And in fact, culinary customs linked to the rural environment still persist today, even in the cities, in various forms. After all, didn't my mother serve us *mămăligă* with milk at home in Bucharest?

There is a sort of storybook image that haunts me, originating, no doubt, in the stories I had heard since childhood about the 'Romanian peasant' who at dawn, before leaving for the fields, would throw three basic foods into his coarse canvas pack, namely, a piece of cold *mămăligă*, a large slice of *telemea* sheep's cheese and a large raw onion.

And this image remains utterly vivid and real to me.

*

Although *mămăligă* is a basic foodstuff without apparent attraction, if one attempts to compare it to a feminine prototype, it makes one think of those unfashionably dressed women who are worth getting to know better, and who, one senses, hide behind an uninteresting and uninviting exterior not only the qualities of a homemaker but even hidden treasures of sensuality. It is rather this type of woman who doesn't excite admiration but who has a presence, whom one can imagine as being a faithful, lifelong companion, not merely one destined for an exciting, passionate but short-lived relationship of which one would soon tire.

45

Yet *mămăligă*, the quintessential food of Romanian cuisine, although simplicity itself, is far from being easy to make. In fact, it used to be considered, and perhaps still is in the countryside, the test that an unmarried girl needs to pass in order to prove her qualities as a future good wife.

A simplified recipe for mămăligă

Pour a large quantity of salted water into a large pot. Bring it to the boil and as it comes to the boil sprinkle it with a little cornmeal and let it boil for two or three minutes. Then pour in the rest of the cornmeal all in one go, stirring vigorously with a wooden spoon or a whisk. Leave to cook on low heat, stirring occasionally. In principle, mămăligă *is cooked when it no longer sticks to sides of the pot.*

This makes it sounds easy, but knowing how to stir the pot is an art in itself, it requires a particular knack, hand movements that are only acquired with long practice especially if you consider the subtleties of preparation, if you want the mixture to be lighter or creamier, or if it needs to be thicker, denser, firmer, without nevertheless losing any of its springiness. The consistency depends on taste or the role that *mămăligă* is destined to play in the meal.

You see, it is a matter of having what I call a true '*mămăligă* instinct' – because basically there is no real recipe for *mămăligă* – one needs to be able to measure the proportions by sight alone in order to obtain the desired effect, because the quality of cornmeal is not always uniform. It also needs to be made quickly, you have to start stirring hard at just the right moment to prevent lumps from forming. *Mămăligă* needs to be cooked for a sufficient length of time but must be removed from the heat just before it starts to stick to the bottom of the pot because nothing spoils the flavour of *mămăligă* more than burning it. The resulting paste should be of a uniform consistency, while remaining slightly lumpy and coarse, at least if the cormeal consists of bright yellow, round grains, the true, authentic *mămăligă* cornmeal of my distant memories.

There are also those little culinary secrets, refinements of a regional character that seem to be almost superstitions, some of which I was unaware of for quite a while. I knew people who would flavour the water for *mămăligă* with a sprig of thyme, or who would throw an unpeeled garlic clove into the cooking water. Others would make the cornmeal creamier by boiling it in a mixture of milk and water — there are infinite variations.

I have more than once pondered on this word, trying to find a meaning for it, some possible interpretations. Is the word *mămăligă* composed of two parts, *mămă* and *ligă*? Thus, *mămă* would be the Mother and *ligă* that which binds, from the Latin *legare*. The roundness of the resulting word would mean: the mother, she who binds, who harmonises, who cherishes us, who keeps us together, who loves us. At least, that is how Romanians feel her warm, reassuring presence, one which is essential, wherever one may find oneself. In any case, were not Romanians once nicknamed *mămăligari*, just as the Romanians call the Italians *macaronari*? This may indicate signs of a deeper identity which needs to be sought far back in time, at the very origins of our history.

Esti's 'Little Dishes': Two hors d'oeuvres that are the foundations of Romanian cuisine

Seventh letter to Agnes

I n the early 1960s, Esti used to go out shopping like everyone else. This meant that, like everyone else, she would stand with endless patience in interminable queues. While this daily grind that one had to endure just to meet one's daily needs, and which was due to the progressive impoverishment of the country, had become a terrible ordeal for a large section of the population, Esti made it into one of her favourite hobbies, almost a social occasion; she went out as if to see a show or a performance and came back titillated, full to the brim with gossip, all sorts of tittle-tattle and the anecdotes that concierges loved to exchange with one another. She would repeat them to us, seasoned with her own comments and interjections, with her usual good nature and that innate sense of humour that she had; we were on tenterhooks each time, eager to hear the next episode.

She would take a folding chair with her and would sit down, listening intently. She would observe, listen, eavesdrop, gauge and judge mercilessly but without malice or rancour. Nothing escaped her. In fact, the little stories she told were often the only thing she brought back because on half the occasions, by the time she had waited for four or five hours, nothing was left. Some people would start standing in those endless queues at three o'clock in the morning, just like young people of today when they are hoping to get seats for a concert given by Madonna or Prince. And don't think that the happy few who had reached their goal returned with who knows what sumptuous booty; there might be a few miserable little frozen fish, or a mangy piece of scrag end, a chicken carcass or, even worse, just chicken feet. People would still be satisfied, this was something for the soup pot, 'they were nourishing'.

That reminds me of a story that used to be told at the time. There was a whole raft of this gallows humour, the result of poverty, the invention of anonymous creators who seemed to have sprung up all over the place. It is the story of a little old woman, carrying an empty shopping bag, who suddenly stops dead in the middle of the street because she can't remember whether she was going to the market or coming back from it! That is just one example of the thousands of bitter anecdotes that circulated *sub rosa*, emanating from that part of the Romanian spirit best expressed in the phrase *a face haz de necaz*, i.e. a capacity or even an irrepressible tendency to joke about misfortune or to make fun of one's own sufferings.

Even if Esti returned from these expeditions empty-handed this did nothing to discourage her. Supported by an optimism that defied every test she found herself so nourished and enriched by the little stories she collected in the market that she had forgotten the futility of her long wait and the initial reason for her trip.

After she had given up these little satisfactions and found herself cloistered in the flat, she turned our home into her world, one which she would slowly pace from end to end, taking small, waddling steps between the two balconies, the front balcony and the rear balcony as we called them, and she was far from unhappy. From then on, these became her 'strategic' look-out posts from which she would sagely scrutinise the outside world.

*

But when all is said and done, it was in the kitchen that Esti spent most of her days. This is where, with an indescribable joy, she created our daily meals and we were not conscious enough at the time of our extraordinary good luck.

50

Without further ado, here at last, my dear, are two complete recipes that I insist on commenting upon for your benefit, as well as a few of Esti's secrets of how to make them and the tricks she used. Let us hope that they will help you to get an idea of the cuisine of my country and to gradually master this particular field. You can find these starters on the menu of every Romanian restaurant, nor will they be absent from the meals celebrated with an unequalled enthusiasm by all the Romanian diasporas throughout the world. You will see that they are very much indicated to guide the first steps of your learning curve. Promise me that you will say their names in Romanian because those poetic sounds that are their original names cannot be dissociated from their flavour, texture and finally the fragrance of these true treasures of Romanian cuisine.

Salată de vinete
(Aubergine Salad)

This is an aubergine purée, of which variations can be found in the numerous so-called 'Greek' or more pejoratively 'Balkan' restaurants, under the irritating name of 'aubergine caviar' which I find pretentious since this is one of the plainest and most ordinary of appetisers. Furthermore, the colour of the dish is not black or even dark grey like caviar. It can therefore be deduced that the term exists purely for commercial reasons to attract a tourist clientele.

The recipe I am giving you here is authentic, I can testify to that, this is the way it was made in our home by Esti and by my mother who, for once, had found common ground, something that was not always the case. This does not mean that other variations may not be encountered elsewhere in Romania. What I am telling you is only based on my direct experience. So this is the recipe to which I can give no name other than *salată de vinete*:

Choose firm aubergines of medium size. Hold each one directly over a flame until the skin takes on the look and texture of a charred crust which can easily be detached in strips. You will know they are cooked if you touch them with a finger and find they are soft and

51

yielding and that under the stiffened, crackled skin, the interior of the vegetable is perfectly supple and soft.

Only then should they be removed from the flame; after leaving them to cool slightly, peel them carefully by hand. If you are in a hurry, you can put them under the cold tap and peel them with a potato-peeler.

When all traces of the burnt skin have been removed, put the flaccid aubergine flesh into a colander or strainer, to drain away the liquid. The aubergines need to release most of their juice, that is important. To do that, you should put the mass of aubergines on a slightly tilted wooden board, put a heavy object on top of them, and leave them to release as much of their liquid as possible.

Take care! It is at this precise moment that the divergence begins between the traditional method used by Esti and the one I am using here, in France, due to force of circumstance, for greater ease of use or simply out of laziness; surely it is through laxity, a lack of thoroughness which I repent of each time I do it. Two methods, two ethics, rather, which may even result in a subtle difference in taste.

While Esti used her own method, placing the aubergines on a wooden chopping board and vigorously attacking them with a wooden chopper, patiently hacking away until the aubergines were reduced to a compact paste that retained its natural, slightly lumpy texture I do the 'civilised thing' and unhesitatingly transfer them to a Moulinex electric food processor. With two simple presses of the button, I see the aubergines transformed into a paste of the smoothest texture. And I know that's not right.

I experience a feeling of unease, as if Esti were watching me behind my back and I sense to what extent she disapproved of what I was doing.

'*No, Domişora*', she would say if she were here, 'that's not the way to do it...'

She would certainly have judged my purée to be too smooth, lacking in character. With a pout of slight disdain, she might even have spotted an undesirable darkening of the mixture as well as a slightly metallic taste left by the blade of the chopper which my manhandled taste-buds can no longer detect.

In fact, Esti's golden rule consisted of never using metal implements, whether a knife, fork or any 'Moulinex accessory', this last being, in any case, completely unknown in Romanian kitchens of the time. That is why for mixing – and she was utterly unshakeable on this point – she would use only a wooden spoon and a sort of chopper, also made of wood, which was used specifically for *salată de vinete*. With time, even I have tended to adopt this rule, although I don't often use the wooden chopper, but at least I stir the mixture with a wooden spoon, thinking of Esti and her advice, the fruits of her culinary wisdom.

And then, you know, between ourselves, the contact of the hand with the tool, the feeling of wood on the skin, is so much pleasanter, more tender. Ah, those wooden spoons, I couldn't do without them. And it is not a matter of their direct effectiveness. No, for me, they are a symbol, they evoke a whole warm, familiar atmosphere, and then they age so much better. Wooden objects become more beautiful with time and wear; I keep a small collection of wooden spoons in my kitchen, some of them have come down to me from Esti, Mama brought them over to me later, when she finally came to visit me in France. There are short ones, long ones, some in pale wood, others almost blackened with use, some have a sculpted handle, the material is steeped in memory, the patina left by a thousand dishes and as many culinary successes or failures. But back to the recipe:

In the next step, the 'first degree' aubergine purée is poured into a large bowl and is then seasoned with salt and pepper. It is now 'swollen' by beating with oil, which is added drop by drop, while stirring slowly with the same wooden spoon, as for a mayonnaise. I have retained the habit of always using sunflower oil, the same oil that we used at home in Romania; olive oil was just a vague memory from before the war, I personally never knew it.

When the purée can be seen to have grown slightly in bulk, add a few finely chopped garlic cloves without skimping on them; this detail provides the whole distinctive taste of the dish. Unfortunately, once again, in my slapdash fashion, I add the garlic cloves right at the beginning, by dropping them into the food processor with the aubergines; it's so much easier that way. Finally, one or two tablespoons of sour cream or crème fraîche gives the mixture a paler colouration and a creamier consistency – this was one of my mother's tricks which she finally managed to get Esti to adopt, not without difficulty. A little lemon juice will lighten the heaviness of the oil.

The last step is by no means the least important, in fact it might even be considered indispensable. This is the 'decorative' part. The result of the previous steps is transferred to a shallow serving bowl. After lightly smoothing the paste with the back of a wooden spoon, it is decorated with rounds of tomato, strips of sweet pepper and black olives, arranged in a flower shape or however you like. I must tell you that Esti and my mother threw themselves enthusiastically into this part of the process and fought for compliments from the diners. Their efforts were always varied and never found wanting. Believe it or not, the decorations were almost more important than the food itself. This handsome product was then consigned for an hour or two to the refrigerator or a cold room because this dish tastes much better if served slightly chilled.

Another very important detail: for Romanians, it is inconceivable to consume this 'classic' starter without spiking the palate with the sharp taste and strong smell of finely chopped raw onion that is incorporated at the last minute, just before the dish is decorated or even served at table on a little side-plate.

*

Fasole bătută
(White bean purée)

This dish is easier to prepare and constitutes the other cornerstone of Romanian cooking in the cold appetiser category. This is how you make it and, here again, I shall discuss two methods, Esti's 'orthodox' method and the 'sacrilegious' one adopted by me through necessity.

First of all, the white beans (dried haricot beans) must be cooked in boiling water until soft, then puréed with a few sliced garlic cloves, salt, pepper and a little of the bean cooking liquid. The wooden spoon is once again brought into service. Do not forget it, it will now become part of the landscape. Once again, Romanians like this dish to be very garlicky and only reluctantly agree to reduce the quantity of this precious condiment, and they utterly refuse to do without it altogether, no compromise can be accepted merely to try and please diners of too delicate a disposition.

Of course, Esti obtained her purée through long and arduous manual labour but I assure you that she took a real pleasure in it. She would use an ancient, hand-operated vegetable mill as an instrument for reducing the beans to a paste.

She would never have stooped to buying canned beans. No, the beans were pure and authentic dried haricot beans that she had soaked the night before and then boiled for an interminably long period. As for me, as you can guess, I use canned beans without scruples, as long as they are labelled 'unseasoned'.

One then continues as for the previous recipe, adding the oil drop by drop so that the volume of the paste can be seen to increase, continuing to stir the mixture until it reaches the desired consistency. It is impossible for me to give you more precise directions here, once again, it is a question of intuition.

A parallel operation is then applied for the next stage because this dish is not enough in itself, at least that is how Romanians conceive of it. It consists in slicing several onions very thinly and frying them in hot oil in a frying pan, slowly and for a long time, stirring frequently with the eternal wooden spoon. I warn you, the onions need to be completely caramelised, turning dark brown, even black in places, without becoming burnt, however. This part is left to last, just before serving at table, because the fried onions must be sprinkled while still warm over a layer of beans deposited in a wide, shallow terracotta bowl.

This typical Romanian appetiser is served warm. Above all, do not refrigerate it, but it should be eaten accompanied by a nicely chilled rosé wine. A jar of chilled pickled cucumbers should also be placed on the table. These dill pickles are sold in jars or cans and are usually imported from the Czech Republic, Israel or Poland. In

Romania, large, fat cucumbers are pickled for many months in barrels of brine, flavoured with herbs, predominantly dill.

This appetiser, like many other dishes made with oil, will keep well for two or three days, especially in winter. I have been told, and I found it hard to believe, that in the past, this dish was considered the food of the poor. It is a native dish with the robust flavours of the country and Romanians everywhere love it unreservedly. But you don't have to be a Romanian to enjoy it, I have concrete proof of this.

So, my dear, that is your first initiation, now you have, as one would say, 'something to get your teeth into'. Practise making them and keep me informed.

A myriad of soups, including *ciorbă* and *borş*
Seventh letter to Agnes

E sti had certain 'strong points' depending on the season, the time of day or the circumstances. While the refreshing aubergine salad, with its slightly acidic flavour, was usually served in summer, the bean purée, which was thicker and heavier, kept one warm in the winter although there is no reason why this basic first course could not be eaten all year round.

At any time of the year, Esti's menus contained soups which, depending on whether they were thick or clear, were called soup, cream soup, *borş* or *ciorbă*. I suppose she got into the habit of giving them special care by calling them by the affectionate diminutive in typical Romanian style, adding the ending *–iţa* or *–eţ*. The result was *borşuleţ, ciorbiţă* and sometimes *supiţă* which satisfied all our appetites. These soups featured permanently in everyday meals, and were never absent at lunchtime.

The cold, even iced, soups and *ciorbe* were there for everyone's enjoyment. Esti would prepare them tirelessly in all their forms and variations of which there were many. My father always requested them. Since then, the only cold soup I have encountered that is similar is the Andalusian gazpacho. Over and above the benefit of their refreshment power, they were also said to be rich in vitamins and minerals.

The great variety of cold soups included the garlicky nettle soup, and the tonic like none other, the *ciorbă de lobodă*, made from a red-leaved herb with a slightly acidic flavour that is unobtainable in France. Then there was the rather bland lettuce soup which was said to be nourishing but which I used to call 'orphanage soup', the rather austere and monastic cumin soup that I didn't much like and the delicious, slightly sweet tomato soup that was flavoured with herbs and tasted of sweet peppers. And finally, there was my favourite – for which I had limitless affection – creamy and light as a kiss, the courgette cream soup made with a dash of milk, which was sprinkled abundantly with fresh dill whose flavour combined divinely with that of the courgette.

In winter, the courgette cream soup was just as delectable when served hot. It could be made thicker and creamier by adding a large lump of butter and a few tablespoons of sour cream. For the cold weather, Esti reserved other surprises for us which extended the range of her soup production. These soups were served piping, even boiling, hot and there were some sublime ones such as the *găluşte* soup, a golden chicken soup, on which pale dumplings floated, the size of a large egg. The dumplings were made from semolina, a little flour and an egg yolk, and bound with egg white beaten into stiff peaks.

These hot soups designed to warm our stomachs in winter were also the ideal remedy to nourish and comfort convalescents recovering from a long illness or simply to alleviate the symptoms of a cold. This substantial liquid also featured on the list of folk remedies of which my mother and Esti knew all the secrets. Esti would use it to pamper us on days when we were a little out of sorts and we sometimes pretended to be ill in order to be given a ladleful or two. We liked it with a few drops of lemon juice and we would dip a few pieces of black bread into it as the sweet warmth invaded our stomachs.

*

It must be acknowledged, however, that a position of the first rank, I would even say the place of honour, was held by *borş*. *Borş* is, by definition, a sour soup, and this one was welcome throughout the year in all its variations. *Borş* is a soup that is made in most of the countries of Eastern Europe, but the Romanian *borş* has nothing in common, except for its acidity, with the borscht, borshch or barszcz of the Russians and the Poles. For us Romanians there are various ways of making it, depending on the basic ingredients. It can be made with chicken or turkey, and even with lamb, especially at Easter; there is also the clearer *borş* in which meatballs are boiled, the *borş de perişoare*, and even a good fish *borş*, such as the famous *borş* of the Danube delta.

The most popular *borş* is, without doubt, the *borş de potroace*, the most beneficial of all beverages served in the early morning after an all-night celebration, something that is not uncommon among Romanians. In short, it is the traditional remedy for a hangover.

It is made from chicken or turkey giblets, in fact the name itself, *potroace*, means 'giblets' in Romanian, but all those other parts of the fowl that are usually despised are also used. All of them are thrown into the soup-pot indiscriminately – wing tips, feet, necks, gizzards, livers, heart – anything goes as long as it adds flavour to the soup.

Even the term *borş* is linked to the way in which the soup is acidified. Unlike other countries in Eastern Europe where this type of soup is often soured with beetroot, the Romanians use the brine in which cabbage has been pickled, leaves of the sour cherry tree or little green grapes picked from the vine before they ripen, those tiny little green fruits of an unbearable sourness – they have a horribly astringent effect on the mouth if eaten raw – which in Romanian are known as *aguridă*.

But apart from these ingredients, the true secret of Romanian-style *borş* is this: to deserve the name 'true *borş* of the Romanians' the sourness should come from a cloudy liquid that can only be homemade and that is obtained by fermenting wheat bran. The name of this liquid is simply *borş*.

Borş was sold in bulk in Bucharest from rather squalid, makeshift, rundown shelters, improvised in the shabby porch of a building. The women selling the bran liquid would write the following announcement in chalk on a piece of board, which was almost always couched in the same wording that had become a sort of classic advertising slogan:

'Aici zilnic borş proaspăt'
(Fresh *borş* here daily)

One would turn up carrying an empty bottle which the seller, who in winter would be wrapped up to the eyes, would fill with this precious substance. She would use a ladle to draw it, slowly and ceremoniously, from a huge jar while making a few comments in honeyed tones about the weather or she might offer some other idle local tittle-tattle. This was the 'little extra' she felt herself obliged to offer her customers, as a good salesperson should.

This native way of souring the *borş* can be got round simply by adding the juice of several lemons. That is how I am forced to do it here, in Paris, another heretical deviation due to absence of 'real *borş*'. Any self-respecting Romanian will tell you that it's 'not the same thing'. In the same passionate tone, he or she will explain to you that what gives it the taste of 'real Romanian *borş*' is the few pinches of a herb known as *leuştean* which must be added just before the end of the cooking. This magic herb is unfortunately impossible to find in France. I still jealously guard a few dried up leaves in a jar that date from heaven knows when. I still use them, and it's as if the fragrance, instead of fading over time, actually becomes stronger. I have written in thick blue pencil on this old jam jar the word *leuştean*.

Sometimes, in a fit of sweet nostalgia, I stick my nose into the jar to smell that warm and unique fragrance that goes to my head, like the odour of the soil.

To cook up a perfect *borş de potroace*, one final indispensable thing remains to be done. The soup must be *dres*, a Romanian word that can be translated by 'adjusted' or 'regulated'. I can see Esti again, adding this final touch just before serving it at table. She removes the pot from the fire and fills a ladle with a mixture of an egg yolk beaten with two heaped tablespoons of sour cream diluted with a little of the hot *borş*; she then pours this ladleful back into the pot. This final gesture gives the soup a slightly milky colour which is enlivened by two large handfuls of chopped herbs, parsley and dill. That is because every Romanian dish worth its salt must receive the benediction of chopped parsley or dill and sometimes both. She would then scoop up a little of the soup into a ladle and, after blowing on it to cool it down, lap it up with lip-smacking gusto and a little sigh of satisfaction.

Personally, I like to add a few turns of the pepper mill to the soup when it is at table. Some people prefer it to taste even more spicy by adding those hot chillies that set your mouth on fire and burn your tastebuds. Depending on the appetite and vitality of each of the diners, thick rings of hot peppers may float in the *borş*. The bravest, usually men but sometimes those tough countrywomen, will crunch these hot chillies with a sort of savage joy and such feats of endurance arouse general admiration. People of that ilk could not even imagine *borş* without the addition of that culinary violence that they cultivate with dedication and a certain sensual delight.

Ode to the aubergine
Ninth letter to Agnes

I t is one of those little pleasures, the games I cultivate that I invent at odd moments. For example, sitting down to write when I find myself 'in the right place', placing myself at an observation post and then writing sort of reports, summaries of my daily life, witnessing what is happening before my eyes down to the details of the most extreme banality, as if they were events of the highest significance; or, on the contrary, letting my mind meander freely among images, observations, memories, reveries... Writing down what passes through my head while preserving the spontaneity of the way in which they have run through my mind.

At this precise moment, on a superb autumn day, at lunchtime, I am sitting on a roadside bench. But it is not just any old road; it is the noble and majestic Avenue Foch which cuts a wide swathe to the horizon.

I turn my face to receive the warmth of the last rays of an autumn sun. Despite the throbbing of the cars – the background noise – that drive past me, I have just finished eating my ham-and-cheese sandwich in milk bread bought from the baker's as well as a golden little madeleine cake. The madeleine is quite good, quickly nibbled... Thus I let my thoughts float as on a cloud, invading me at will.

And suddenly, I don't know why, I begin contemplating the sculptured aubergine. Heaven knows why, the aubergine, with its magnificent deep violet colour, the smooth brilliance of its skin, the elegance of its shape, as perfect as the bodywork of a sports car, this handsome vegetable which can be unjustly described as 'ordinary' has haunted me for several days.

The aubergine is used extensively in Romanian cooking where it occupies a place of honour; I venture to say that its taste is often associated with that of garlic. And, one thing leads to another, and this brings me to my mother. I can well understand why. In our household, she reigned supreme over the 'aubergine domain', she knew the largest number of recipes for cooking it, the most diverse ways of seasoning it and preparing it so that we, the family, could enjoy it all the more. I must say that she showed a particular affection for certain vegetables, of which the aubergine was one. No doubt that is why she reserved an exclusivity over its use in cooking.

But why does the aubergine in particular, and only the aubergine, put me in such a turmoil of emotion? Mystery and again mystery. After all, what moves me about the aubergine is perhaps its total destruction, the way it is chopped into tiny pieces the way the purity of its original shape must suffer for the purpose of cookery. But no doubt, that is its fate.

Like everything living that is destined to perish, with its presence, its personality, it effaces itself with a wonderful humility, accepting the renunciation of such a perfect, noble shape, in order to overwhelm one of our senses, that of taste, having turned into that soft, easily digestible food that comes into direct contact with our taste-buds, melts in our saliva, revealing unsuspected riches and making us forget its original appearance.

*

How can one be unaware of that irreplaceable feeling of comfort caused by the heady fragrance of grilled aubergine, the flavour – a mixture of smooth and spicy – of its cooked flesh, harmoniously combined with other fragrances and the taste of spices and other suitable accompaniments? More specifically, a family feeling, the warmth of being 'at home'. Surely it must go back a long way? Was there a specific moment when the fragrance, that of cooked aubergine, fried or grilled, reached my childish nostrils or even when I was a baby – anything is conceivable – and that this moment was associated with a feeling of such intense pleasure?

But to return to the subject, as I said, it was in fact Mama, my mother, who was the 'aubergine specialist' in our house. Due to her penchant for this vegetable, there was not a single one of the innumerable ways of preparing it of which she was unaware. Apart from the aubergine salad that you know already, and which tended more to be within Esti's domain, there was, to choose just two outstanding examples, *musaka* and *imam bayaldi*, names that are filled with 'all the perfumes of Arabia', evocative of the lasciviousness and sweetness of the Turkish harem, masterpieces of the culinary heritage left behind by the fierce Ottomans who oppressed us for centuries, whom I imagine to be dark, very brown, moustachioed, dressed in outlandish costumes and cruel as devils; between ourselves, if the only thing they had bequeathed to us was Turkish coffee I would have been ready to pardon them at least some of their misdeeds.

As for *musaka*, my mother was the real expert. Even Esti, who was hungry for compliments, was prepared to grant her precedence here. Mama later gave me the recipe but although I have tried it out more than once, I have never really succeeded. Here it is, however, as I noted it down, you might have more luck with it than I did.

*

Musaka

Heat some oil in a frying pan and cook a chopped onion in it until lightly browned. Add a mixture of minced meat consisting of one-third pork, two-thirds beef and cook it with the onion. You can also incorporate a grated carrot and a grated potato. Cook on low heat for a while, mixing from time to time and adding a little water. Then remove the mixture from the fire and break two eggs into it. Mix well, season with salt and pepper and sprinkle with a few handfuls of chopped herbs, such as parsley, dill and celery leaves.

Separately, choose a few smooth, firm aubergines of average size. Trim the stalk ends and slice them crossways into rounds the thickness of a finger. Parboil them for a few moments in salted water, then arrange them on a slanting wooden board and sprinkle them with salt so that they release as much of their liquid as possible. Wipe each of the slices separately with kitchen paper. Dip each slice in flour and fry them lightly in batches in very hot oil, without cooking them completely.

Oil an ovenproof dish, and fill it with alternate layers of aubergine and minced meat, finishing with a layer of aubergines which you then cover completely with rounds of tomatoes. To finish, sprinkle the whole with a few ladlefuls of hot water or stock and bake for about 1 hour in a hot oven.

Ten minutes before the end of the cooking time, combine one or two eggs with a tablespoon of flour and two tablespoons of sour cream. Beat well and pour the mixture over the contents of the ovenproof dish. Return it to the oven and cook for another ten minutes, or until the top is lightly browned.

Before serving, sprinkle the dish with chopped parsley, you will note the stimulating contrast, indispensable for sharpening the appetite, of the bright green in contrast to the tender red of the tomatoes. A nicely chilled rosé or a red wine would be welcome to awaken the most intimate aromas of this everyday but nonetheless succulent dish.

We were in the habit of accompanying the *musaka* with a mixture of yogurt and sour cream which was placed on the table in a pot, so that each diner could sprinkle the mixture over the contents of his or her plate. That is a fairly common Romanian accompaniment to stuffed vegetables and sauced dishes.

Recipe for *imam bayaldi*

I think that for most ordinary people this dish is easier to make. This is what you do:

Trim the stems from the aubergines. Wash them and split them in half lengthways without peeling them. Plunge them into salted boiling water for a few moments, then drain them carefully and stick a few peeled garlic cloves into them.

Cover the bottom of an oiled ovenproof dish with a layer of sliced tomatoes. Sprinkle them with chopped parsley and a few chopped celery leaves. Then arrange the aubergine slices on top, cover with another layer of tomatoes and sprinkle with oil. Bake until the tomato juice runs and the aubergines become golden and slightly crunchy, without being burned.

I personally prefer to eat this dish cold as a starter. It will keep well for several days if an irresistible desire suddenly seizes us and we devour a mouthful at first light.

I end this ode to the aubergine by hugging you, my dearest.

A little more about Mama's cooking
Tenth letter to Agnes

On some Sundays, the house had the clean smell of vinegar and polish. In those days, there was nothing but vinegar and washing soda, or even ashes to make a house spick and span; the innumerable brands of detergents were something that no one had ever heard of... For the washing up, Esti used a rag soaked in washing soda or a little ash. That is why her hands had become so red. As for the laundry, all we had was 'washing soap', a block of the coarsest mixture of fat, ashes and lye.

*

On the days when she found the time, usually Sundays, Mama would launch into sustained cleaning sessions. Armed with a rag impregnated with vinegar, she insisted on doing all the cleaning and polishing everything herself. This included cleaning those ancient, ragged Turkish carpets whose harmonies of colours and patterns were so sublime. Then she would dust, rub, polish, and pat her engraved copper vases, her embroidered cushions, her Bavarian porcelain and her silver cutlery, some of which had been repaired. She did this in the same way that she performed every task she set herself, with vigour, vitality and a sort of joy tinged with candour as well as that poetic quality that was hers alone.

With respect to the sheer physical effort involved in housework, Mama was perfectly happy to apply the sort of advice my father gave us when he took us on those long hikes into the Carpathians.

When we complained of feeling tired, he would advise us to 'rest while walking'. She applied this advice to her everyday life, without effort and without premeditation. She rarely rested, and if she did it was in order to stitch embroidery or do some reading. She would tell us that it was from this that she derived all her energy and youthfulness.

She was a doctor and biologist by profession and spent many hours at work, some of it at the hospital and, at one time, she also did lab work in a makeshift laboratory that she had installed in a room in our flat, yet she still found enough energy to indulge wholeheartedly in those activities which were her hobbies. One of these little, parallel occupations, was the annual jam-making sessions. More frequently, there was what she called 'the Sunday clean', Sunday being the only day of rest in the week.

I can picture those sunny summer days, when the windows and balcony doors would be thrown wide open 'so that the house can breathe' as she used to say, when she devoted herself to polishing, frenziedly rubbing and then putting everything back in its place with a care inspired by her attention to detail and innate sense of decoration. There was nothing pedantic in these tidying sessions, but rather what I would call a poetry of the imperfect which she practised quite unconsciously, happy to periodically perform a new inventory of the treasures she had accumulated, not for their value but for her own pleasure, for the flights of fancy they allowed her. She dedicated a whole cult to them. She was never tired of staring at them and examining them, taking a sort of childish pleasure in them.

At the end of each of these housework days, the house gleamed with happiness and the harmony that was re-created each time, as if by a miracle, among the miscellany of objects and bric-a-brac furniture. This innate sense, this gift for colour that Mama expressed every day around us was something of which she was not even aware. No one doubted that it would emerge again much later and much more apparently when she suddenly took up painting, after the death of my father in the early 1960s.

*

70

But by far the most important of my mother's hobbies was cookery. It was not easy for her to use this gift because it often involved beng in direct competition with Esti. These confrontations could be of a redoubtable nature.

For my mother, cookery was much more than a mere leisure pursuit, it fell somewhere between an occupation and a hobby. She was really gifted although her approach tended to be that of an artist. Towards the end of her days, she talked to us of a dream she had always had of opening a restaurant. With her precious gifts of vitality and her talent for hospitality, she would have been quite capable of doing so.

It was in the evening, especially at the evening meal, that she concentrated her culinary energy most particularly; she did so during the period when she was close to retirement when Esti was growing old and had lost some of her strength. Mama had accustomed us to two or three main variations of this light, easy cookery which was her favourite field. Because, since she was a dietician before it became fashionable, she advocated the principles of light, easily digestible food.

Of course, *mămăligă* featured at the head of the list of Mama's evening menus. We ate it at least two or three times a week. Yet my mother preferred a 'different' *mămăligă*, one which she called *mămăligă pripită*, ie. quick, fast, spontaneous, and thus less firm, more airy. By using more water and less cornmeal, the mixture needed to be stirred very fast and continuously with a wooden spoon or even with a whisk, before it was simmered on a low heat until it could be seen to be detaching itself slightly from the sides of the pot.

Mama served it for preference with the ewe's milk cheese known as *telemea*, in classic Romanian style, or again with a curd cheese from the country. In both cases, sour cream was poured liberally over the dish, not forgetting the hearty, homely raw onion to be crunched with it.

At the table, my father would ask for a large, peeled raw onion, one of those huge purple bulbs, to be brought to him; he claimed that this type had softer flesh. After sprinkling it with coarse salt, he would wrap it in a napkin and place it on a corner of the table. He

71

would then deal it an almighty and particularly skilful blow which was intended to soften it. It was a single blow, but a well-aimed one, bang! The table shook and we all watched him closely. This was the time-honoured method of rendering the onion flesh softer and its flavour milder. We never understood why, but the flesh of the onion, worked and softened by the force of my father's fist, tasted almost sweet, and my father claimed that even little children could eat it. That was the honest truth. This barbaric gesture, no doubt of rustic origin, made an extraordinary impact on us and had a sort of obvious symbolism, as the stamp of my father's authority. In fact, it was common practice, not only in the country but even in the town, in many families who, like ours, lived close to those old traditions that they attempted to perpetuate with a fresh good humour that added spice to the atmosphere.

Sometimes this soft, spontaneous *mămăligă*, whipped up like a sort of sketch, was accompanied by a simple fried egg or an omelette. Mama was a master at this recipe which we loved. She would thickly butter an oval Pyrex dish and pour the *mămăligă* into it while it was still steaming hot. She would then leave it to cool slightly and then, with the back of a spoon, make a few nest-like holes in the golden mass, into each of which she would slide a raw egg. She would then dot the dish with butter and sprinkle it with grated cheese – gruyère or *telemea* – and a little sour cream, before sliding it into a hot oven. After about half an hour, I think, or at least long enough for the eggs to be cooked through and the surface covered with a delicious crunchy, golden crust, the dish was ready. Before serving it, she would pour a little more sour cream over it.

My mother knew quite a number of these baked *mămăligă* variations and she made them for us with renewed pleasure each time, a pleasure that we eagerly shared. Look, here's another one which consisted in alternating, in a buttered ovenproof dish, successive layers of *mămăligă*, butter, *telemea* cheese or a full-fat, yellow cheese, a little like the aged cheddar-type cheese that shepherds would wrap in fir tree bark which steeped it in the fragrance of a whole forest. This is the famous *burduf* or *brânză de burduf*. You ought to have seen this cheese melt in the oven so exquisitely, so mouth-wateringly, enveloped in the warm mass of *mămăligă* which captured all the wonderful smells of the oven floor and finally emerged resplendent, as if embroidered on top and carpeted under that amber-coloured, crunchy topping that we quarrelled over at the table because all of us wanted to have the largest piece of it. My mother would scrape the bottom of the Pyrex dish down to the last crumb so that the whole table would get equal portions.

I could not finish this brief survey of the simple dishes that Mama made for us in the evening without mentioning the famous omelette which will remind you a little of the Basque dish known as *piperade*, but without the ham. She made it exclusively with vegetables – tomatoes, sweet peppers and above all a large quantity of finely chopped spring onions which are used extensively in Romanian cooking. She would always keep the trimmings from spring onions and would use them extensively in other dishes, since they provided flavour to stews, omelettes and salads.

To begin with, she would chop the green parts of the spring onions and fry them in oil in a frying pan. Then she would add sweet peppers cut into strips and lastly coarsely chopped tomatoes. When the tomatoes had softened, she would season them with salt and pepper and add a large handful of fresh herbs, such as dill and parsley. Then she would pour in the eggs, which had been beaten with a little milk and a pinch of flour to give the omelette more body.

I often make this omelette myself for improvised dinners, when friends arrive unannounced, unexpected guests who are content with any improvisation. Because the omelette can be varied with all sorts of ingredients, it is the ideal way of using up leftovers. Anything that comes to hand is welcome – pieces of cheese, mushrooms, remains of cooked meat, cooked potatoes, courgettes, aubergines, slices of sausage and who knows what else. The result is an incredible range of flavours with subtle differences which can be varied infinitely.

Not long ago, you tasted one of those omelettes and you said it was extremely good. I never tire of the 'Mama-style' omelette or what I call the 'old pals' omelette.

My Father
Eleventh letter to Agnes

S nuggled up to this stable point, the interior warmth of the home that a happy childhood bestowed upon me as a gift, I nevertheless found myself inhabited at an early stage by an inexplicable desire to transgress the limits, or even to know another side, to go and see what lay 'beyond'. It wasn't a question of running away, but to move away so as to better 'reposition' the permanence and comfort of 'our home'.

To leave so as to return all the better, to reposition myself better. From the beginning, around the round circle of familiar tastes and smells, cosseted, cared for, pampered with an unequalled devotion and the same amount of talent by Esti and my mother, gradually, like parallel circuit, the routes and other excursions that led me into the areas of difference, the domains of 'the other', as much 'other' as I liked to periodically rediscover or that I would encounter by the always welcome chance of circumstance.

Leaving, travelling, never stopping. This need to move, this desire to go away, to be ready to pack a suitcase at any moment if the occasion arose, taking the train, the boat, the plane, without despising going on foot. More than a caprice, this passion, almost a vice, came, I'm sure, from my father. I would also unhesitatingly designate him in the role of master and initiator for everything that concerned travel and departures.

My father was an engineer, a builder of trains and he pursued his occupation with passion, as a true vocation; in this he was directly marked with the 'house of travel', a term used in astrology. More than once, he took us by the hand to visit stations, his favourite places, magical places, to let us admire a belching steam locomotive ready to trigger its amazing and superb mechanism that he would lovingly contemplate. It was a love that he would so liked to have transmitted to us but unfortunately, our choices lay elsewhere.

For long time, his favourite reading matter concerned the prodigious lives of the great explorers who were moved by this thirst for the wide open spaces, for travel and discovery. They were extraordinary people whose names still haunt me – Nansen and Amundsen were his idols. He would read incessantly about their heroic lives. From his early youth, at a time when people did not travel a great deal and holidays had barely been invented, father had already declared himself to be a tireless traveller. He had traversed the length and breadth of the Carpathians, nor did Turkey hold any secrets for him and he and a few friends had even climbed Mont Blanc, equipped like true mountaineers with ice-axes, crampons and ropes. As evidence, I still have the old tattered photo albums, full to bursting with the yellowed images of these trips, near or far, black-and-white or sepia photos that he took himself.

Just before he married my mother, he was getting ready for a trip around the world. But fate decreed otherwise; he fell irretrievably in love and decided to make the terrible sacrifice. Instead of distant horizons, he chose my mother's beautiful eyes, assuming that he would be able to take up his alpenstock at a later date, in her company. That is what he must have told himself, without knowing that 'the later date' was not to be, for shortly thereafter, the frontiers were sealed by the Communist regime, and it was goodbye to foreign travel. Even less did either of them expect this situation to last for several decades. One single chance was all they had left, their honeymoon, which took the form of a trip through Europe – Italy, Germany and then France, places so distant and mysterious for us children that we could not imagine ever being able to go there ourselves one day.

The story of that time, bathed as it was in an amazing happiness, which had acquired an almost mythical dimension, was constantly recounted to us until we knew even the most minor incident by heart, whether it was picking oranges from a bush, a wine with the poetic name of Lacrima Christi (Christ's tears), or a suitcase forgotten at the Berlin train station but quickly recovered, and we never tired of hearing them.

We were a well-travelled family. Of course, our trips had to be within Romania because as soon as the frontiers were closed, foreign travel entered the realm of the myth and the fairy story. But this pronounced taste for travel was also stimulated by the fact that my parents, both employees of Romanian Railways, benefited from perks which were also available to their children. Furthermore, they were dedicated to worship of nature and to holidays. The Carpathian mountains, the Black Sea, charming provincial towns such as *Râmnicu-Sărat* where my parents were born, or *Pucioasa*, a little spa town which was the home of my aunt, my mother's elder sister who was married to a lawyer, were just some of the places where we spent part of our holidays.

*

At a very early age, I manifested the violent thrusts of an instinct for seeking freedom that was innate in me and which was to explode much later, even though I was only knee-high to a grasshopper, annoyed at something my parents had forbidden me to do. I packed my little suitcase, a sort of doll's suitcase into which I remember very well having thrown two or three knicknacks, a doll and a ragged teddy-bear, and I started down the staircase. Of course, I didn't get very far and my parents, while scolding me, soon caught up with me on the first floor, that is to say, only one flight down. No doubt, this *wanderlust*, this longing to travel – this way of never wanting to stay put – is something I must have inherited from my father. Was this not the main motivation for the decision I took thirty years ago never to return to Romania? I know that it came from a deeper impulse, the rejection of the barrier that had been imposed on me, the frontiers I was forbidden to cross – and this absurdity was something I found impossible to accept.

We children called him *Tata*, meaning 'father' in Romanian. My mother bizarrely called him 'John', in commemoration of their first meeting at an English class, when they were both students in Bucharest. My mother was studying medicine, a brave, almost scandalous choice for a girl in the early 1920s, especially one from a middle-class family in a small provincial town; the man who was to become my father was studying engineering at the Polytechnic.

Despite a repressed aggression of which no one but his closest associates was aware, my father was as reserved and withdrawn as my mother was voluble, quick-tempered and extremely generous. If my father, on rare occasions, dared to utter a few timid words of reproach on the rather spendthrift side of my mother, she would react immediately, calling my father a miser! At other times, she would be overwhelmed by the proverbial distraction and dreamy side of my father who, according to her, did not have 'his feet on the ground'.

Needless to say, these arguments, which were violent but short-lived, passed like summer storms. I even believe that these little, fairly frequent spats, not only failed to spoil the closeness of a couple who had the deepest affection for each other, they may even have had a beneficial and stimulating effect on their relationship.

It was generally my mother who gained the upper hand. In everyday life, one indeed got the impression that, to coin an old Romanian saying, 'it was the hen that crowed', in other words, she wore the trousers. This translation does not quite convey the situation, however, because my mother's authoritarian nature in no way detracted from her femininity. In any case, it was Father who took the important decisions in times of crisis. That was obvious. My father was someone who spoke rarely and little; and only when absolutely necessary. His anger had more weight because it was rarer and thus more concentrated. On the other hand, poor Mama would over-dramatise, she broke into a rage over nothing, which obviously diluted the effect.

*

If I ever have to write my gastronomic memoirs, Mama and Esti will play the leading roles. Yet the picture would not be complete – and I am speaking generally about everything connected with taste and smell – if I did not add a few anecdotes about the wit that was my father's. He had a certain dry humour, gestures, puns or even tics which among his own circle had been given the name of 'valerisms' from his name, Valeriu.

Father took no part in cooking but his relationship to food is one that deserves to be dwelt upon because, as in a painting, these are the details that bring a whole tableau to life. I would merely mention this very special affection he had for unsuccessful, even burnt, cakes. Dishes that 'hadn't worked' inspired a sort of tenderness in him, as if he wanted at any cost to save them from the contempt of heartless people and those who, I would say, had no poetry or humour.

Famously, as soon as he smelled burning, he would cross the kitchen threshold, or rather sneak in, and start scraping the bottom of a pan, with a sort of avidity he would rather have kept secret, to remove the carbonised remains of a *plăcintă*, say, doing so with mischievous gluttony, regardless of the mocking laughter of Esti who admitted to being completely flummoxed by this behaviour. He would imperturbably reply with a witty remark, a brief and original allusion, but a telling one, which made everyone laugh but him, because he was well-known for that impassive expression that he always maintained when making a joke, just like Buster Keaton to whom he was compared and whom he idolised. He would then adopt a slightly embarrassed look and there was just a tiny gleam in his small black eyes that he would screw up slightly in order to wordlessly translate his inner amusement. You ought to have seen the seriousness and immobility of his expression amid the general hilarity that he had just provoked with so little effort, sometimes with a mere trifle... He could have made a career as a humorist, I always used to say so to myself.

At table, my father would sit with a slightly bowed back, as if folded in upon himself, his spectacles on his nose, in an attitude of intense concentration that was all his own. I was always fascinated by the meticulousness, the perfect elegance, even grace, of the way he ate. He seemed to treat food with a kind of respect, a delicacy and at the same time, a mathematical thoroughness. Unfortunately, I have never been able to do the same. At the end of the meal, his plate was a wonderful sight, always ordered, cared for, like a valuable object, especially when it was fish, whose bones were carefully placed around the plate, 'arranged' in categories with a pedantry that did not exclude a certain aestheticism.

Yet despite the elegance of his simplest gestures, he was in no way an esthete. In fact, I would say that my father was more 'down-to-earth' and more of a nature-lover than Mama. It is he who took us to places in the country that were rather rustic and primitive while Mama wanted to keep us away from them. He had been a bachelor until the age of thirty-five, taking as long as possible to 'settle down' so that he would have every freedom to enjoy a rather rackety existence, with its unpolished charms, free and unattached, consisting of meals on the run and much frequenting of rather uncouth places, such as the taverns, 'low dives' known as *cârciumă* in which a lady wouldn't be seen dead. The men gathered there to carouse, far from a dignified and well-ordered family setting, in a jovial, noisy atmosphere punctuated by bursts of raucous laughter and salacious stories. In these places, the food consistent of succulent but rather heavy dishes, local food with hearty, spicy flavours which was one of the reasons for going there, to these almost secret places and, needless to say, the eats were well washed down with plenty of drink. At least, that is how I have always imagined them. Yes, my father probably retained a nostalgic, secret longing for that time in his life that he always recalled with evident regret. Is this again something I have inherited? I myself have often had a certain taste, close to fascination, for the sort of place that can be found almost anywhere, in France and abroad, if you look hardest for them, and I have always preferred them to fancy establishments, with their pompous, starchy atmosphere for which even the refinement of the food cannot compensate.

Father loved the atmosphere of country fairs and would take us to them whenever he got the chance. These places seemed to us to be exciting and mysterious and we always returned to them with delight, titillated by the temptation of the forbidden, in this instance personified by the authority of my mother, who was rather a stickler for 'what will people think?' There was no question of going there too often, it wasn't 'respectable'. And once again, my father played the role of initiator in these secret and impromptu trips to that shady and dubious setting.

There we were in the midst of the multicoloured crowd, at the lively *tiribombă* and various other shooting galleries. The fairs were usually run by gypsies, marginal people with whom respectable folk did not mix. Yet it was so easy to succumb to the all-embracing charm of these nomads who had come from distant, troubled horizons. They had the well-established reputation of being petty thieves and liars but no one could remain indifferent to the mysterious attraction of their dark beauty, their proud and distant facial expressions, their eccentricity, the royal insolence of their gait, as well as their extraordinary talent as self-taught musicians, an art they practised with a mixture of spontaneous inspiration and over-acting. It was indeed due to that whole excessive and disreputable gathering that we experienced a frisson of liberty each time we had the opportunity of rubbing shoulders with gypsies, of meeting them in passing.

My father and I shared the same childish joy, despite our age difference, in the excitement of these excursions which finally became accessible to us after numerous negotiations with my mother; she always gave in eventually. When I recall the smell of those sausages grilling on the dirt-encrusted barbecue grills set up next to the gypsy caravans, my mouth still waters. I would easily have succumbed to the temptation of running away with them to wherever they were going. These smells evoked a whole exhilarating atmosphere that drew us to them and we would have gone with them to ride in their caravans, jolting along among their copper knicknacks and brightly coloured bits of cloth. At the time, these sausages, of very doubtful manufacture that were so despised by my mother, melted in my mouth, after titillating my nostrils with their intoxicating fragrance. Once again, the smell was redolent of a whole world. The 'product' was lavishly seasoned with burning mustard that took the skin off the roof of your mouth. But as a well-behaved little girl who took great pleasure in slumming it, I bore this attack with a heroism of which I was quite proud and swallowed my tears. At the time, I found this bad quality food mingled strangely with an inexplicable and confusing feeling, the vertigo of freedom. And then, there were the gypsies with their amusingly cheeky humour, who were so good at advertising their dubious wares, sometimes shouting out naïve doggerel to describe them, that our curiosity and our tastebuds were stimulated irresistibly, just listening to them talk.

These secret outings were thus one of those little sins that were only partially permitted and I was all agog for the next occasion. Upon returning from these trips, my mother, and Esti even more so, with a pout of disgust, insisted on our removing our clothing, eager to dispel that acrid smell that had penetrated us to the bone. Finally, to be frank, I felt myself linked to my father in a sort of tacit complicity.

From the world of the gypsies, with whom I imagined my father had hidden ties or with whom he was at least on familiar terms, he would bring home certain habits of consuming such snack foods as boiled or grilled corn-on-the-cob. We would munch them directly from the cob after coating them with butter and rubbing them with coarse salt. At other time, he would come home with maize grains which he would put on the fire until they burst into *floricele* or 'little flowers' which I later discovered under the very American and commonplace name of 'popcorn'. Sometimes, it is enough for a food to be eaten under different conditions for it to seem like something completely different. Thus, the Romanian *floricele*, no doubt more primitive, grilled by my father or sold by gypsies in the street, seem to be totally unrelated to the popcorn sold in the cinema foyers on the Champs-Elysées, which were industrialised products spat out by vending machines.

In Bucharest, beautiful gypsy women, swaying provocatively, monopolised the trade. They would sit on the pavement, spreading their wide, brightly-coloured skirts, and tempt passers-by with their dark, wild beauty, displaying their brilliant white, animal teeth in a tantalising smile as they offered *floricele* or corn-on-the cob – *porumbielu' cald...*', 'Piping hot, piping hot, this little cob'. They would bring out the corn cobs from large baskets in which they kept them wrapped in dampened hot cloths. Oh, the fragrance of those corn cobs, we could smell them from far away and would rush over to fill our hands and crunch them on the run...

My Father's Culinary 'Innovations'
Twelfth letter to Agnes

I t was always my father who came home last from his job. Mama did not always have the patience to wait for him and would have already eaten. She would take advantage of the fact to sit in front of him and start to bombard him with questions, animated by a very feminine curiosity. She would ask what had happened at the office and about his health and then took her time to tell him about various little stories or incidents from the hospital where she worked, rumours and a few items of gossip, and so on and so on.

Father would imperturbably continue to concentrate on his meal which he would carefully dissect with his usual patience. He would say little and seemed to attribute little importance to these stories and the insistence of the questions into which my mother poured all her convictions. As if in a trance, he would reply disconnectedly and only in monosyllables, which infuriated my mother and often she would eventually stop, murmuring a few reproaches. Then he, who had been merely waiting for this defeat, was finally able to relax and calmly devote himself to eating with an untrammeled relish.

For a long time, I attempted to discover, behind the scientific professions of my parents, a few vestiges of the creative spirit that could have predicted the destiny of their offspring. For, to the extreme surprise of my parents, my brother in turn also chose an artistic career. My mother had a taste for beautiful things, she had an innate sense of colour. But my father? I think he had dabbled with paintbrushes in his youth. One day, I discovered among his things a miniature set of paints and I told myself that he must only have painted mini-atures. Music tempted him as well; he would scrape away at a violin with a delicate, timid bow, almost mutely 'so as not to disturb the neighbours' like almost everything he did. In the evening, after din-ner, he would remove his violin from a shabby, black box as slowly and carefully as if it were a Stradivarius, and he would ask me to ac-company him on the piano in a simple air such as the Turkish March in a simplified version or a transcription of an Italian canzonetta. He would also play these popular tunes to us on His Master's Voice records, turning the handle on an ancient wind-up gramophone.

Yet these hobbies could hardly be described as creative. On the other hand, in his own calling he had shown himself to have the gifts of an inventor, having even succeeded in patenting a few little innovations always connected with trains.

I told myself that part of his ingenuity was manifested, curiously, at table. In eating, he excelled in the act of feeding himself which was magnified, sublimated by a creative impulse that was triggered at the very moment of mealtimes. And it is as if he was pursuing research work, through experiments which he seemed to perform frequently with the intention of each time improving the contents of his plate so as to turn them into some new product that he had patiently perfected with genuine pleasure, quite remote from any futile desire to get himself noticed. And he would leave the table doubly satisfied.

Among the few culinary inventions that he persuaded us to adopt, because he loved to proselytise, there was what we would call 'Father's aubergine purée'. The difference was subtle because, without altering the recipe for this hors d'oeuvre radically, he would produce a dish of indisputable originality which was enough in it-self. This is the recipe and how he did it:

Once Esti had placed in front of him at table the usual dish of **salată de vinete** or aubergine purée, he would consider it as his raw material. With that careful and precise gesture which he was so good at, he would begin by skinning a tomato, a simple tomato; you would think he was creating a sketch at the same time. Then he would cut it into tiny pieces which he would set himself to slowly

84

crushing with a fork. He would then mix the crushed tomato with the aubergine purée and season it lightly with a splash of vinegar and crushed pepper. A finely chopped onion was incorporated without hesitation for, in any case, my father was a big eater of onions in all their forms. The result thus obtained, which was spicier and more strongly flavoured, with a more marked character, was spread on thick slices of black bread. He would then take his time in consuming this work of art with a sort of interior pleasure that would make his little black eyes sparkle. That's all there was to it. It doesn't sound like much but this little discovery became a delight that was unanimously appreciated.

He even introduced variations. I preferred the one that used grilled sweet peppers in a salad. Esti would often serve it to us at table, especially to accompany the aubergine salad. The peppers were cooked directly over the fire, peeled and served cold, sliced in strips, sprinkled with a spiced vinegar and lots of chopped garlic. My father would cut the peppers even more finely and mix them with the aubergine purée. These little culinary rituals took on greater importance for him than even the meal itself. No point in saying that for this reason, the meals became particularly lengthy – he was almost always the last person to leave the table – but these habits had become indispensable for him and no one dreamed of blaming him. This was his way of expressing his individuality, of inventing his own world, something he must have felt a need to do.

The green colour of certain breakfasts
Thirteenth letter to Agnes

D uring the week, I often make do with lunch of an apple and a yogurt, sometimes eaten with a rusk. That's enough to keep me going until the evening when I eat more copiously, at home and in peace. It has taken me some time to get used to this rhythm.

How different to the Romanian lunches, those daily meals without trimmings or pretentions; these were really hearty meals, eaten at leisure. In our home, it was Esti who provided them unfailingly and regularly with all her skill and devotion and a constant care to vary the menus to offer each of us our very specific favourites to fulfil our love for specific foods and our hungry mouths.

The splash of green of the spinach or nettle purées were often repeated. Esti would serve these greens more than once on the daily menu. As a 'painter in the grass' from the earliest years, I already enjoyed distinguishing between the subtle range of shades, from the warm dark green of the spinach to the brighter, coarser, more violent green of the nettles. I can see again the kitchen table covered with that mass of fresh greenery, ready to be cleaned and judiciously peeled by the expert hands of Esti. For us, it was the height of amusement to see her put on gloves to peel the nettles, a spectacle of surrealist fun; Esti stood there with her corpulence, dealing with the nettles in her gloved fingers, her glasses falling off the end of her nose.

As soon as the cleaning operation was completed, the nettles were plunged into a big pot of boiling water. Esti would then drain them and flavour them with milk or sour cream and a nut of butter; but above all, she would put in lots of garlic to attenuate their strong smell. Thus prepared, these smooth, tasty nettle purées, and the spinach purée made in the same way but with a milder flavour because the garlic was absent, were admirable accompaniments to fried eggs or the parents of poor knights that we called *frigănele*. These were no more nor less than slices of white bread, the so-called *franzelă* (French bread) which was comparable to a baguette, although of much poorer quality. Esti would dip each slice of bread into milk, then into a beaten egg, and she would fry each one separately in butter in a frying pan. They went just as well with garden peas or lightly sugared sautéed carrots. Curiously, we would always sprinkle the *frigănele* with a little sugar and even served like that they were the highlight of the meal. Despite its being such a humble dish, it took on the allure of a delicious desert and it was adored by the children; it was eaten hot but could even be eaten cold the next day if there was any left over. So it became a light desert for the evening, or a teatime snack; then it just needed to be sprinkled with a little more sugar, cinnamon, or to spread the slices with apricot or strawberry jam.

Among the images that surface from my memory of early childhood I can see myself when very small sitting at table before a plate of 'spinach *frigănele*'. As usual, I had difficulty swallowing it, I am a small eater. Every ploy was used by the family, including sentimental blackmail, to make me swallow each mouthful of food which I would always retain in my cheek for a long time, to the general despair. (Yes, dear Agnes, the healthy appetite that you recognise in me did not develop until much later, when I was about fourteen). Suddenly, my ears resonated to a strident sound, one that was inconceivable, followed by other terrifying noises. These were the air raid sirens and the first bombs that fell on Bucharest. Seated at table in front of me was *nenea Luca*, the colonel, the bachelor uncle who was my mother's elder brother, who used to eat with us at the time. His hands trembled and his voice was shaky as he tried clumsily to reassure me and I could feel his unease. I was surprised that a grown-up could lose his cool in that way. Later, I learned that Uncle

Luca had been shell-shocked, having been 'buried with a bomb' during the war. I did not understand what that meant but I knew that it must have been terrible for him and he inspired waves of compassion in me.

Standing on the threshold of the kitchen, petrified with fear, Esti was crossing herself with expansive gestures.

That is just to show – fleeting thought – how a peaceful splash of green can sometimes evoke violent memories.

Chiftele, plăcintă and other ways of preparing meat
Fourteenth letter to Agnes

A s for meat, I have to tell you that we did not have much of it, no more than twice or three times during the week and never twice a day. This was not just due to the meat shortage, it was an entrenched custom, no one found a need to eat meat every day, at any price. That's how it was. Roast joints of meat were totally unknown to us. As for the 'grills' that Esti would sometimes make for us, they were extremely overcooked and had the consistency of shoe leather; she would serve them drowned in their own cooking fat. I can now confess that I never liked Esti's custom of cooking meat 'Transylvanian style', smothered in oil or lard in a frying-pan. But these gaps in her cookery skills were so rare that I never mentioned them to her. I always put the failing down to the quality of the meat, and in this there was certainly an element of truth.

For delicious, crunchy, melting grills, flavoured with aromatics and herbs and grilled over a wood fire, the only option was a restaurant. Kebabs and shashlik would be consumed in a jovial, good-natured atmosphere, often to the accompaniment of a little orchestra or a gypsy violin at *grădina de vară*, the open-air restaurants that can be found on every street corner in Bucharest. There, you could order a nice pork chop, filet mignon or entrecôte steak, and especially the famous *mitiei*, typically Romanian kebabs, consisting of short, thick sausages made from a mixture of chopped meats, flavoured with herbs and fragrant spices, that were continually basted with a marinade containing raw garlic as they cooked. This is not an easy thing to do and good *mitiei* can rarely be eaten outside a restaurant.

At home, meat was usually cooked in a stew, a ragoût or some sort of fricassee, of which there was an endless list, using chicken, beef or lamb. Many other dishes were inspired by a whole series of recipes that were clearly of Balkan, Turkish or Greek origin and that relied heavily on minced meat, used especially as a form of stuffing. There were all sorts of such dishes, beginning with stuffed peppers, then stuffed tomatoes and even stuffed potatoes, as well as stuffed courgettes, stuffed vine leaves and finally, *musaka*. The meat used as a stuffing would emerge from Esti's mincing machine, when she turned the handle, in a thick red sausage. The metal mincer was one of those antique objects that she manipulated with the skill of long practice. The meat was generally a mixture of beef and pork to which rice and spices were subsequently added. It was used to stuff various hollowed-out vegetables.

Apart from stuffed vegetables, Romanian cooking has two essential preparations based on minced meat. These are *chiftele* and the famous, succulent *plăcintă*.

One cannot speak of Romanian cooking without mentioning *chiftele*. These meatballs are encountered in various forms in every region of Romania. They are made of a mixture of minced meat, about two-thirds beef and one-third pork – but you can also improvise – and the meat is combined with a richly seasoned mixture that is rubbed through the fingers for a long time in a bowl preferably made of earthenware – this is another recipe that requires carnal, physical participation – as one incorporates a succession of ingredients that are required if the desired consistency and aroma are to be obtained before the mixture sputters in the pan:

Recipe for chiftele

minced meat
soft white breadcrumbs, soaked in milk and squeezed
one or two whole eggs
finely chopped onion lightly fried in oil
(although one of my friends uses the onion raw)
a lot of chopped herbs, especially parsley and dill
as much, if not more, chopped garlic

Combine the ingredients and when the mixture is sufficiently homogenous and smooth when rubbed with the tips of the fingers, sprinkle a work surface with a thin dusting of flour. Take small amounts of the mixture in the palm of your hand and shape it into meatballs, then roll them first in the flour, then in the palm of the hand, to slightly flatten the balls. Drop them, one by one, into a frying pan of very hot sunflower oil so that they bubble and splutter. Cook them until they are brown and crisp all over, ensuring that they are well cooked and soft inside. Of course, there is nothing to stop you from tasting one of the first to be ready – purely to check to see if they are cooked – they are delicious when eaten on a slice of bread.

Using this basic recipe, the possibilities multiply, because *chiftele* lend themselves to infinite subtleties of interpretation, as regards flavour, consistency and shape. They also vary according to region, family and even from one individual to the next. Infinite variations or even major changes can be made in the ingredients, the amount of time they are allowed to cook, and the little improvisations introduced by individuals to give them a 'soul', a personal touch.

They can be served hot or cold, the large ones as a main course, tiny, even almost microscopic ones, to be added to the swift succession of *gustări*, the selection of canapés served before the hors d'oeuvres to be consumed with a drop or two of *ţuică*.

In Moldavia, the *chiftele* are bigger, the size of a large egg, oval and crunchier because they are first rolled in dry breadcrumbs or even in cornmeal instead of the usual wheat flour. This variation is commonly accompanied with mashed potatoes and a green salad flavoured with dill and garlic, plus a little squeeze of lemon juice, a dash of salt and a sprinkle of oil. They can also be served in a tarragon-flavoured tomato sauce when they are called *chiftele marinate*, are eaten hot or even cold. I am only quoting a few of the numerous possibilities for serving these meatballs which are a 'key element' of Romanian cuisine.

At home, Esti served them to us in all sorts of guises, for it was she who made them most perfectly. She was even famous in our circle of friends for her *chiftele*. Ah, Esti's *chiftele*! When she prepared them, the delicious smell of their cooking, the way they sizzled in the pan, would immediately attract one to the kitchen. One of our small pleasures was when she gave us a 'foretaste', a *chiftea*, just out of the pan, so piping hot that she had to blow on it to cool it down, just before sliding it, on a morsel of bread, into our wide-open mouths. It was her way of feeding her chicks.

An all-purpose pie – the great *plăcintă*
Fifteenth letter to Agnes

La plăcinte înainte
la razboi inapoi
(Forwards for *plăcintă*
Backwards for war)

I am quoting an ancient Romanian proverb comparable to the famous and hackneyed slogan of the hippies 'Make love not war'. My father never failed to utter it, as if for the first time, whenever Esti decided to make one of those delicious flaky pastry pies called *plăcintă*, using dough that she made herself. This home-made dessert required particular skill and she knew all the tricks and smallest subtleties. *Plăcintă* is something like an English pie or a Moroccan brik. It tops the list of adaptable dishes, whose range of possibilities can be transformed according to circumstance into an hors d'oeuvre, a main dish or a dessert, and can be served hot or cold depending on the filling. I would call it a 'miracle pie' or 'all-purpose pie'.

'Little mother, it melts in the mouth!' Our guests would exclaim, licking their lips. This was the compliment that Esti had been waiting for, demanded even, as a reward for her patience, her admirable finesse, the precision of movement that she used in order to achieve a truly elastic mixture, the ineffable transparency of a sheet of dough, the exquisite, melting flavour of the filling.

For her *plăcintă*, Esti always made her own sheets of dough. This almost mediaeval custom was a true feat, but still widely practiced at the time. I remember her locked in hand-to-hand combat with the ball of dough which she would beat vigorously and at length on the kitchen table, then roll it out, brandishing her rolling pin like a sceptre, spreading out the huge sheets as thin as wedding veils yet flexible and strong. In order to prove to us that her *plăcintă* dough was a success, Esti would drape it over her outstretched arms, holding it against the light from the window, to demonstrate and prove to herself the perfect consistency and elasticity of her masterpiece.

Today, I doubt there is a single woman alive who could boast of performing such a feat, unless she is a masochist. That is because you can find the dough in shops everywhere, in Romania or in England. It is phyllo dough that one can buy in any Greek or Turkish neighbourhood. In France, in Balkan groceries, it is known as '*plăcintă*' (or a similar-sounding variation) and in North African groceries it is called brik. You will find the dough, frozen or fresh, in sheets rolled up on a thick sheets of release paper. Esti would have despised this solution, but it is hard to turn one's nose up at it today. Each packet of dough contains twenty or so sheets that can be kept for several weeks in the refrigerator and even for several months in the freezer, as long as it remains unopened.

To make *plăcintă*, you delicately detach the sheets one by one, draping them over a rolling pin and spread them out, brushing each in turn with melted butter. They are then arranged in successive layers in a buttered and floured pie dish of suitable size, preferably one made of earthenware. When five or six layers have been laid in the dish, this featherbed of dough is covered with a filling of your choice, sweet or savoury, which is then covered with another layer of sheets of dough of the same thickness as the first. Using this basic recipe for *plăcintă*, you could devise the menu for a whole meal, since it would be easy to adapt it into an hors d'oeuvre, a main course or a dessert. Here is yet another of these miracle foods that the Romanians love to invent.

For savoury *plăcinte*, which always taste better hot, served as hors d'oeuvres or as *gustare* (canapés), there was one that was filled with ewe's milk cheese which Esti sometimes liked to dot with cumin seeds; but her real vote-winner was her meat *plăcintă* which was more substantial and spicier, and served piping hot. It was made with minced beef and, if served with a green salad, it could easily do for a main course.

In addition to these basic variations, there were others, all of them her specialities, though she made them less frequently. Each was more delicious than the last. There were pies filled with leeks, mushrooms and even pumpkin.

For the sweet *plăcinte*, the most frequent variation was curd cheese and raisins. This is the one that is most frequently found in Romanian cooking.

Plăcintă cu Brânză
Recipe for Plăcintă *with Cheese*

Macerate a good handful of raisins in dark rum or strong tea overnight. Take about 500 grams (18 oz) of well-drained curd cheese and fold six egg yolks carefully into it. Then beat the egg whites into stiff peaks and fold them into the mixture. Drain the raisins and add them to the mixture.

Esti always flavoured this creamy mixture with a little grated lemon rind. She would finish the pie by brushing the top sheet of dough with beaten egg, then sprinkling it with icing sugar. She would then bake it in a hot oven (220°C/450°F).

The *plăcintă* was cooked, of course, when the tip of a knife inserted into it came out dry. Personally, I prefer to serve this pie very hot. Shortly after removing it from the oven, it should be cut into slices which are arranged on a large dish and then dusted, if liked, with a thick cloud of icing sugar.

Some people prefer a different variation, the apple *plăcintă*, which is lighter and more fragrant, flavoured with vanilla sugar and cinnamon. Sometimes a few chopped walnuts or raisins are added, and it then bears an uncanny resemblance to a Viennese apple strudel. It is eaten hot or cold, thickly dusted with icing sugar.

I don't remember seeing these *plăcinte* in public places, such as restaurants or bistros, except perhaps the savoury *plăcinte*, filled with meat or ewe's milk cheese. On the corner of our street, there was a shabby little café, too small for the number of customers who patronised it, which sold nothing but a delicious savoury *plăcintă* and beer. The pie was served straight from the baking dish and was cut into generous wedges which were eaten standing, accompanied by a foaming pitcher of cold beer. Esti found it hard to hide her jealousy whenever she found us hanging around this *plăcintărie*; she considered such excursions as infidelities, almost elopements. We found these sorties into the realm of simple fare to be quite attractive, but we did all we could to get her to forgive us, swearing that her *plăcintă* remained the finest without any doubt, which was in any case, the pure, unvarnished truth.

Water-melon and its role in high summer – cool places
Sixteenth letter to Agnes

Just like every other morning, I walk through the market in the rue de Lévis to catch bus no. 30 in the Boulevard des Batignolles. I stroll among the stalls, that joyful bounty of fruit and vegetables, fresh and brightly coloured, so succulent and sparkling clean, as if displayed for a festival or a fashion show; they are a little too carefully arranged for my taste, too orderly, calling too much attention to themselves.

I stop for a moment, as I usually do, to leaf through the books in the Librairie Fontaine whose trestle tables are out here in the street, in front of the shop, next to the tomatoes and the artichokes. Then, pensively, my gaze dwells for longer than usual on the pale pink, anaemic-looking slices of water-melon, pitifully wrapped in clear plastic. Water-melon always reminds me of the great Romanian heatwaves of my childhood.

It's hot, a rather sticky heat, but attenuated, not too aggressive. Bearable but irritating. We are a long way from the Romanian climate which is continental and dry, consisting of pronounced and even excessive contrasts. The winter is bitterly cold and frosty with snowstorms. In the dog days of summer, it's like a furnace, the sun burns so hot that we can feel the asphalt softening, burning and melting beneath our feet.

Fortunately, these spells of torrid heat were punctuated by heavy showers. Then, mad with joy, we would paddle barefoot in the middle of Bucharest, allowing the streams of water to flow through our hair and down our arms, open to the generosity of the powerful rainstorm. I have always loved storms, floods, that feeling of release…

*

Apart from the rain, that gift from the sky, very fortunately there were other remedies and sweet delights to tame the heatwaves. In the evening, a pleasant breeze would waft in like a balm; the taverns would then fill up with a diversity of patrons, who had come to quench their thirst with a cold beer or a *șpriț*, popular tipple in Romania, especially in summer, consisting of squirting soda water from a siphon (*sifon*) into a glass of wine; the term was used to indicate both the contents of the siphon and the siphon itself, the turquoise glass bottles that were so decorative and that were to be found in every home. They could easily be taken down to be refilled at the local bistro.

Purists never failed to criticise the *șpriț* as a way of spoiling wine, considering it to be a sacrilege, but it was part of a well-established folklore, a verse or two from the poetry that was specific to the city. In fact, most people would never have considered drinking wine in any way other than as a *șpriț*. After all, these were not fine wines and valuable vintages but simple, drinkable, ordinary, everyday wines.

*

At nightfall, we would set out on long walks in the direction of the lakes that surrounded Bucharest like a cool ring of freshness. We would stroll down the wide avenues edged with red rose-trees, sometimes losing ourselves in the paths shaded by linden trees, their large leaves and heady blossoms filling the air with intoxicating fragrances that made us dizzy, a season like no other for falling in love; we would continue at leisure among the rows of sweet chestnut trees that contained myriads of glow-worms who signalled to each other secretly and brilliantly in the darkness, the dim street-lighting making their light even more intense. These evening strolls 'along the avenue' as we called that other world that opened up at night was, and still is, a real tradition in Bucharest, almost a rule of life. We would see courting couples, elderly ladies and even a few solitary dreamers; we would go there to seek some cooler air and peace and quiet, as well as to take exercise – because you would cover two or three miles with ease – just to be alone, to find a romantic atmosphere, look at the stars and simply smell the fresh air.

*

Water-melon was the supreme way of cooling down during the excessive heat and this august fruit became indispensable, the cool sweetness of its flesh mitigating the harshness of the weather. The irreplaceable water-melon, so generous, juicy and voluptuous…

Do you want to know how to choose a good water-melon? This is an art in which my father excelled. And in fact, choosing a water-melon was man's work, because these Romanian water-melons attained monstrous sizes with a weight to match. They were said to be even better if they weighed ten or twelve kilograms (between 22 and over 26 lb), real phenomena! Male muscles were therefore welcome, not only to carry them home from the market but also to choose them and even to cut them open. We children often had the opportunity of witnessing these preliminary gestures because we would happily accompany my father to the market to watch the water-melon buying proceedings.

Like the true connoisseur that he was, my father began by testing the water-melons. He would weigh them up, press them very hard close to his ear between his palms, until, as he explained it to us, he heard a faint cracking noise; this sign was the indubitable proof of the fruit's internal qualities. Like a surgeon palpating his patient, my father would bring his ear close to the firm, smooth, dark-green skin. My little brother and I would stand there, holding our breath, as we awaited his verdict:

– 'This is the one, this one is good!' He would declare firmly. And he was never wrong.

101

And then we went to weigh it. The peasant who sold them would use his big hands to manoeuvre one of those old-fashioned weighing machines in heavy, rusty iron, adding and removing weights of all sizes to make up the weight – and finally we would find out the exact weight, ten kilos, or even12 kilos! It was important to be able to announce the weight when we got home.

When it was time for dessert, we all gathered around the table, almost reverentially awaiting the cool melon which arrived, carried in ceremoniously on a large tray by Esti. Esti, the pixie of the hearth, the good fairy.

*

The operation would be performed in several stages. First came the initial cut across the top of the sphere, the 'cap'. This was the only horizontal cut and we knew that it would offer us, an initial glimpse of the contents of its huge entrails. In a few moments, piercing deep into the belly of this sturdy fruit, the shiny blade of the knife would reveal its colour; would we see that acidulated rose-red or the paler orange shade?

Armed with a well-honed knife, my father would hold the enormous mass of the water-melon in one hand, to balance his weight, while in the other he would dissect it, this time vertically, with a powerful gesture. We waited spellbound as if for the curtain to rise at the theatre. Each time, the flesh of these water-melons would offer us the most delicious spectacle of colour which varied extensively, from the frivolity of a bright red, through various shades of pink to the unusual orange tones or, as an exception, the rare treat of a pale yellow. And there were plenty of 'Oh's' and 'Ah's' of wonderment as we beheld the sight.

My father would then move on to the next phase by detaching huge slices, one after the other, which he would distribute fairly. The first of them, dotted with shiny black seeds, would split from the fruit like a cry. It would be offered around first to retain the sweetest and most delicious essence, concentrated in the top, the *cocoş* which means 'cockerel' in Romanian, since it looked so much like the bright red of a cockscomb. This was the very heart of the water-melon.

Only the children had the right to first taste of this delicious treat, a sliver of this exquisite part offered on the point of a knife. We were permitted, on such an occasion, to pick it off with our fingers. We often abandoned knife and fork to bite deep into the slice, our faces happily buried in the juicy and beneficial substance. In fact, after having bathed in this beneficent juice our cheeks became smooth and shiny like the skin of a baby and, quite apart from the refreshing effect, we felt lighter and cleaner. A feeling of wellbeing would overcome us and we had the impression of breathing more easily.

*

Water-melon took pride of place over everything else, at *Râmnicu-Sărat*, in my grandfather's house. Things were done differently there, the circumstances were not the same and we even had the impression of not tasting the same water-melon. As soon as the hot weather started, grandfather ordered a delivery from the surrounding countryside of huge mountains of water-melons which arrived in a *căruță*, the Romanian peasant cart drawn by two horses. As soon as they had been unloaded, the water-melons were taken down to the *beci*, a deep, crudely built cellar dug into each courtyard in the country and provincial cities. Access to this dark, mysterious place was awkward, one had to use the narrow steep flight of steps down to it whose treads were worn and uneven. These cellars were used for storing most foodstuffs and were used permanently for every sort of winter provision. We did not go down there often due to the lack of safety. In any case, the children were not allowed down there and no doubt to deter us, we were frightened by stories of rats, spiders or bogeymen who, we were told, sometimes ventured in there and hid somewhere down there, right at the back, in the dark. So only grandfather and *Miţa* were allowed to go down into the *beci*, lighting their way with a candle or a torch, on a real expedition.

Miţa had been with the family since before my mother's birth and occupied a similar role to that of Esti in our family. I vaguely

remember her deadpan humour and a large black wart that decorated her chin. When grandfather and *Miţa* felt their way down into
these depths, we would remain outside, near the entrance, silently
inhaling the musty odour, the acrid, spicy smells that were peculiar
to these cellars that seemed to us to be the very embodiment of
mystery, of a hidden, slightly malevolent world by which we were
intrigued. They would emerge again their arms full of the most banal ingredients, a few potatoes wrapped in newspaper, a couple of
bottles of *ţuică*, dried beans and, of course, a water-melon, its skin
misted from the cold. And we would return to reality.

*

Although there was the *beci* or a much larger and better equipped
cellar known as a *pivniţă* in the country or in the provinces, each
city flat possessed a tiny storeroom called a *cămară* that served as a
larder and was cool and damp. We had one in our flat in Bucharest.
It is here, on the wooden shelves of this little room, reached from the
corridor that linked the dining room to the kitchen, that Mama stored
provisions. Our *cămară* contained enough provisions to open a gro-
cery. It was used for storing what we termed as 'dry goods', a habit
acquired during times of famine, when people went out buying all
sorts of items, especially food, as soon as they appeared on the market, even when they had no immediate use for them, and storing
them, due to the permanent fear of being without. But many home-
made preserves were stored in the same place. Our larder contained
bottles of oil, vinegar, glass jars of preserves of all types made by
Esti and Mama at various times of the year, especially the famous
murături – pickled vegetables which added their flavour to all sorts
of dishes – with the accent on pickled gherkins, but there was also
a type of round, red sweet pepper, known as *gogoşari*, marinated in
vinegar; or the tasty *gogonele*, green tomatoes in brine, a speciality.
There was at least one good row of carefully arranged bottles filled
with the famous *bulion*, which was merely a locally made tomato
concentrate, essential for any dish cooked in sauce; not forgetting a
whole battalion of pots of jam of various origins and flavours, then

herbs and aromatics in brown paper bags and potatoes weighing down large baskets. The store-room was thus better supplied and more fragrant than an oriental *souk*, you could find almost anything there and I loved to poke my nose inside it, to inhale the exciting richness of these aromas that had a sensuality about them that was typical of the Balkans.

But I see that I am straying from the subject. Moving away from water-melon, where do I find myself? It doesn't matter, let's leave these fragments of memories as they rise to the surface of their own volition, let us follow their meanderings to see where they lead…

The endurance test of the Carpathians
Seventeenth letter to Agnes

Whenever I think of my father, astonishing images and scenes pass before my eyes as if in a film. But those that first come to mind with amazing brilliance are no doubt those connected to our 'excursions' into the Carpathians where I used to spend one month's holiday every year with my family. The long hikes in the company of my father appeared to have nothing to do with food. For me, they evoke perhaps in a truer way, the foods of the earth in their original, raw aspect that I consider to be less worthy of respect. These lengths of time spent in the company of my father, alone in the Romanian mountains, remain for me associated rather with a prehistory of cookery. It was 'raw food' that predominated, rather than the 'well-cooked'; a time to return to one's origins to forget complicated, over-civilised food that had long simmered on the hob, to say goodbye to sauces, marinades and soups; like the troglodytes, we attacked our food with the same delight in its simplest form, chewed on it in the open air, close to the roots of trees and the wildwood…

*

I was barely a month old when I first breathed the pure air of the Carpathians, when placed outdoors in my cradle. This was at the little resort of *Buşteni*, at the foot of the mountain, where my parents were in the habit of renting a house; I was lucky enough to be able to return there every year since my birth and until the beginning of my adolescence. It was a good start in life…

At the time of these long treks through the mountains which remain so intensely linked to the image of my father, I was only six or seven years old. My little brother was still a baby and remained 'down below' with my mother who was not very athletic, while my father and I had the privilege of going 'up there', like explorers. My mother occasionally joined us, before the birth of my brother, for rambles that were even longer, lasting two or three days. Nights spent in shelters that had the bare minimum of comforts, isolated in the mountains, exhaustion, the satisfaction of sustained effort to reach the landmarks before nightfall, gave me a feeling of exaltation, of a real expedition...

But I preferred by far those wilder days, spent alone in the company of my father. We would set off early in the morning surrounded by the rituals at which he was so adept. From the day before, I waited impatiently for the moment at which he chose to start out. Day had barely broken and, while trying to make as little noise as possible so as not to wake the others, we set off before six o'clock in the morning.

My father had filled his 'rucksack' – the English term was used in Romanian – with provisions for the day. He would bring along a chicken, some raw sausages, bread and some fresh fruit. Water in a gourd, a few biscuits and a bar of chocolate completed the menu. The sparkling purity of the air, the perfect calm, the sharp, exhilarating scent of the trees, captivated me from the first steps. On the sage advice of my father, it was forbidden, at least at the beginning, to wear oneself out unnecessarily by taking steep short cuts; this sort of false courage was for beginners. We took care to move slowly, along a simpler, safer path, one step at a time, without hurrying but stopping as little as possible, and taking care to breathe correctly. Birdsong broke the vast silence of the forest whose presence we felt as if it were a person, and we had that sharp awareness of being alone in the vastness. It was grandiose. When I think about it, I retain the image of a lost paradise that I never stopped trying to rediscover later in life.

*

My father was a great sportsman – he claimed to have tried every sport in his life 'at least once' – and these long rambles through the mountains had no secrets for him. Despite the long time gap, I seem to see him again, so close. Like a true professional, my father took pleasure in initiating me into the rudiments of mountain hiking. He is here, next to me, his presence gives me confidence; he holds my hand and hands me down the secrets of the forest and of mountaineering. When we reached one of the peaks, we would admire the vast panorama, the breathtaking view, the blue mountains stretching to infinity on which, even at the height of summer, one could still discern traces of snow.

He also taught me how to examine nature close up, to discover species of plants, to wonder at their splendour and their delicacy. He would show me the hiding-places of the tiny wild strawberries with their heady perfumes, raspberry bushes whose fruits were engorged with sweet juice; or the rare specimens of edelweiss, those strange flowers whose thick petals look as if they had been cut out of felt , which only grow on bare rocks in places that are difficult of access; it is a perilous exploit to pick them, and that is why they are pressed and preserved in albums so that their memory can be maintained. The light, diaphanous, mauve, bell-shaped corollas of the campanulas preferred the shade, dewdrops lingering on their petals.

My footfall became accustomed to the rough contact with the grass, bare earth, gravel and rock. My legs were scratched by brambles and covered in insect bites. Even my hands and arms sometimes bled when I brushed against thorny stems while we were picking the wild harvest but I know that is the price to be paid because the best raspberries, the largest and the ripest of them, always grow on the topmost branches that are the hardest to reach. All this, warmed by the heavy summer sun that awakened the moist odour of vegetation from the depths of the earth and the lively, fresh scent of alpine flowers.

It was then that I felt born within me this pronounced love of nature in the raw which my father had bequeathed to me and which I would retain forever. At the age of six, I would climb the steep slope barefoot, like a little mountain goat. He was proud of me and found it amusing to nickname me 'the savage' or even 'Toura, goddess of the jungle'. A little dog-eared photo of the period shows me, scantily dressed, with a bold air and proud expression, I was in my element. My head was protected from the burning sun by a little scarf and I have a rope around my waist, tied by my father who did so out of caution 'so as not to lose me on the way'.

These expeditions sometimes took steep, narrow, tortuous paths which were madly adventurous, and we would hack our way, as in Gulliver's Travels, through gigantic clumps of ferns. Towards the end of the morning, the sun began to beat down hard. Then my father gave me the instruction: we could take off our shoes and strip down to a bathing costume. Since then, I have had a real passion for walking around barefoot, one of those little pleasures that I retain as second nature and that I cultivate whenever I have the chance, outdoors, in the countryside, or even at home in the house. I love to feel that intimate contact with the earth beneath the sole of my foot.

*

More than once, we were confronted with the difficulties of mountaineering; to successfully complete a steep climb we had recourse to precarious measures, we would hang on to branches as much as possible and to the tips of rocks that might crumble beneath our fingers at any moment. The risk, the dizziness of danger exhilarated me, I would feel an exquisite shudder run through me. It is then that my father would grasp the rope around my waist with his firm hand to stop me sliding, for the slope was slippery and hard. But there were times when I would disobey, untie myself and run away, urged on by the breakneck spirit that possesses me. One day, which I shall never forget, I was trying to pick a magnificent flower that had a huge stem covered in tiny-fuchsia-coloured corollas like a chandelier. But it was growing just out of reach. While he was supporting me, my father slipped on a patch of gravel. For a few instants, I was unsupported, on the point of falling into the abyss, I was almost clinging to a void, and could imagine my fragile body

110

being smashed against the jagged rocks right at the bottom. My head was spinning and I thought I had had it. Scolding me for my lack of caution and what he used to call my 'exploits of an adventuress' my father had to climb down to 'extract me from the ravine' and set me on the right path.

In those days, there were no clearly signposted paths, the territory was almost virgin and unpolluted and not disfigured as it is today by the detritus that tourist vandals leave behind in their wake. The sun splashed the deep shade of the forest with pools of light. From time to time we stumbled upon bright meadows sprinkled with clouds of giant marguerites as tall as my shoulder. In the shade of large trees, among the brambles, beside a cool, babbling stream, there grew clumps of myosotis, the forget-me-nots which have the same common name in Romanian ('*nu mă uita*') as they do in English; this flower has been my secret superstition ever since.

*

Towards the end of the morning, I would begin to feel serious pangs of hunger in the pit of my stomach. But my father had decided that we must not stop for anything before we had reached a certain peak that he would point to over there, in the distance, but which grew ever closer. He would nevertheless grant me a few short stops on the way allowing me to summarily restore my strength, while waiting for the actual meal, thanks to a few biscuits, a square of chocolate, a gulp of cold water drunk straight from the aluminium water-bottle. This water-bottle was part of his 'excursionist's' equipment as he liked to call it. There was also a full set of tableware – plates, glasses and cutlery, all made of aluminium; before plastic, this was the most modern material of the time, practical due to its light weight, the best and most up-to-date implements to be found.

The term 'excursion' that my father used seems to me much more appropriate than 'ramble' which for me evokes a sort of feeble loitering or prim family stroll. For me, it has nothing of the pungent, vital aspect, tinged with wild adventure that lent spice to these delightful getaways.

The long-awaited moment when we could eat finally arrived in early afternoon, but never earlier, and only when we had attained our goal. Utterly exhausted by fatigue and hunger, all I wanted to do was to flop down on the bare earth. But the desire to rest and satisfy a genuine hunger was forgotten in an instant due to my impatience to be involved in the preparations for the Big Meal, a repast in the forest masterfully orchestrated by my father.

As usual, it was my tricky task to collect twigs for lighting the fire. Fully aware of the importance of this responsibility, I was careful to follow my father's advice and choose only the driest pieces of wood so as to be sure to be able to ignite the Great Fire. For his part, with the assistance of an impressive and well-sharpened penknife, a Swiss one to boot, Father cut the branches that were to serve as the framework, that cleverly arranged pile of branches, which would bring the fire to life. The final gesture consisted in cutting a branch into a special shape, to be used as the turnspit. This final element was a sort of 'icing on the cake', it needed to be chosen carefully and its discovery filled me with joy. As for my father, he accomplished all these tasks with consummate art and, needless to say, he filled me with boundless admiration.

Once the first flames shot up from the fire, the chicken, impaled on the improvised turnspit, was ceremoniously balanced by a firmly supported counterweight, carved to measure; faced with this sight, even before smelling the aroma of the chicken, my salivary glands were stimulated to a paroxysm, merely in contemplation of the fowl whose meltingly tender flesh in contact with the embers began to exude the deliciously sublime aroma of roasting meat.

Thus, in the silence of the forest, our sense of smell, or even all five of our senses, were sharpened even further. We listened to the crackling of the roast as the drops of fat fell into the fire and I inhaled the fragrance of the chicken as I watched it take on that wonderful golden colour with here and there a blackened crust that I would like to have munched without further ado. The odours of the cooking mingled with the heavy scent of the leaves engorged with dew, the raw fragrance of the green moss that unrolled like a thick carpet at the foot of the trees which launched their vigorous massive trunks towards the sky as if to impale it.

It was at that precise moment that my father pronounced the magic words so long awaited, 'The chicken is cooked at last'.

Then from the moment he handed me the first piece of chicken, so golden and crunchy, the rumblings in my stomach that had reached the limit of bearable, were immediately reduced to silence. I cannot tell you how it tasted, since sublime would be too feeble an adjective; it was incomparable, this chicken, exquisite, delicious, divine, it would make any person melt who had even an almost normal appetite. Can you understand? I admit it; no cuisine, however sophisticated and perfect, ever gave me such gustatory pleasure and made me feel so replete. It goes without saying that the chicken was literally devoured, with fingers, with elbows, with eyes and with chin, in total abandon, bringing out all our long-suppressed instincts, and even more so, our ancestry.

We needed to refresh ourselves and wash away all the impurities, a necessity that imposed itself after gorging ourselves so barbarously, but this was easy thanks to the numerous springs that flowed all around, close by. My father, who was both a wizard and a water-diviner, had a gift for finding them. He continued his task of educating me about nature, this time teaching me how to use my hands to collect the perfect limpidity of this water which I gulped down greedily, quite freely letting it run down my parched throat. Its cold purity was such that I could immerse myself in it completely.

But on these Tarzan-like escapades we were not deprived of a dessert. Other delights awaited us, and these were by no means lesser. Of course, to complete the meal with the appropriate touch of sweetness, we had deep purple plums and muscatel raisins that my father had brought with him in his knapsack. Yet by far the most delectable, beyond the slightest doubt, were the berries picked from the branches. Bowed down to the ground by the weight of their unusually heavy fruits, the spiny branches of the raspberries exuded that heavy, humid warmth which portended their being engorged with juice. Their heady perfume melting on the lips combined with the feeling of irritation I had from being scratched by so many thorns and brambles, and the stinging nettles that we found it hard to avoid.

At other times we discovered, like so many surprise, the tiny wild strawberries, the bright red droplets with such a delicate and intense flavour, that cleverly hid themselves under luxuriant clumps of ferns or in the deepest shade at the roots of gigantic fir trees whose tops were too high for us to see. These escapades took us further and further from our encampment, but were like a game in their spontaneity, awakening in us the most lively enthusiasm and curiosity. We were so carried away that we risked getting lost along pathways that became ever narrower, invaded by thick undergrowth through which Father, as leader of the expedition, opened the way using his penknife. As for me, I never wanted this exciting half-picnic, half-adventure, to end.

Yet, we were gradually overcome with fatigue. Returning to the place where the fire was gradually dying down to its embers, full and replete, I dozed in the shade, under a blanket, before starting homewards. Evening was about to fall and 'down below' another world awaited us from which we had been cut off for a whole day. It had the features of my mother, slightly anxious and perhaps even a little jealous.

Desserts, puddings and confectionery
Eighteenth letter to Agnes

As if in a forgotten drawer stuffed with old photographs, pieces of ribbon, yellowed letters and discarded fragments, I rummage and sniff this jumble of scents, sensations and images that haunt me. They mingle and separate out without any apparent logic and I let them overcome me.

Here is Esti, youthful and sprightly, having been hired to work for us just before my birth, as I saw her in photographs. Then suddenly, here she is old, her skin flabby, dozing weakly in an armchair in the dining-room. Was this before or after I left, the image that I have constructed when thinking about her so often?

Here again, Mama is vigorously polishing her copper pots on one of those bright Sundays. She stops for a moment to signal to me to go and get some *frişcă* at the *cofetărie*. I deduce that she intends to make a cake. To translate this into English, I am supposed to go and fetch some whipped cream or *frişcă* – which used to be sold in bulk at the bakeries that are also teashops and are known in Romanian as *cofetărie*. The name *frişcă* probably comes from a German word introduced, no doubt, through the Austro-Hungarian influence along with a number of those delicious pastries which were Esti's particular speciality, due to her Transylvanian origins. This Austro-Hungarian incursion into Romanian cuisine is an addition to the long list of other influences which have inspired and given body to our culinary culture throughout our history, to end up in an incredible richness of a 'melting-pot of cultures' – Turkish, Russian and Greek, just to name the main ones, not forgetting the French influence which has also been quite considerable.

My mother assiduously maintained the custom of using a profusion of whipped cream in her desserts, inspired by the whole atmosphere that once surrounded the finest Romanian cuisine, embodied in restaurants such as *Capscha, Ambasador, Cofetăria Angelescu* and *Nestor*, legendary pre-war havens of culture and elegance, in many ways the equivalent of such famous Parisian cafés as Les Deux Magots or Café Flore, which earned Bucharest its nickname of 'Petit Paris'. Without nevertheless aspiring to call themselves 'literary cafés', they were nevertheless frequented by artists, writers, intellectuals or a certain section of the middle class that hungered for culture. For a long time, these places managed to preserve an undeniable prestige and, even under the Communist regime, the ineffable trace of a certain aura inherited from times past still lingered, despite the inevitable decline in the atmosphere and customs and the dilapidation of the décor. People had retained the habit of sometimes spending the afternoon tasting the famous *parfait au chocolat* at Nestor.

To return to the reason for the *frişcă*, it was my mother who used most of it in our house due to her great talent for so-called 'elegant' desserts, those that were rather elaborate, often filled with an abundance of chocolate, crystallised fruits and other delicious things, which required a nicely fluffy topping of whipped cream. She used this superfluous cloud, the frivolity of which was indispensable, especially for her 'king of desserts', the famous *tort de bezea*, a monumental confection which required painstaking and complicated preparation, since it consisted of numerous, superimposed layers of meringue; she would bake these meringue rounds herself, one at a time, then spread them copiously with rich, thick chocolate cream, finally enveloping everything in a luscious, feathery coating of whipped cream. 'With ingredients such as these', joked my father, 'how could it taste bad?'

This mythical gâteau, the apotheosis of dessert, was never absent on our birthdays, it had become synonymous with them and we waited impatiently from one year to the next so as to be able to enjoy them once again.

As for 'mundane' desserts, so humble that we had even forgotten their origin, those simple, everyday puddings, the making of these devolved upon Esti and her know-how needed no advertisement. Even before Mama started getting interested in making desserts, we awarded Esti, who gave in to our childish jokes with that compliance and largesse that belongs to generous spirits who alone know how not to take themselves too seriously, the pompous title of 'doctor of desserts'. And I would happily award her this degree even today. She retained her title for a long time until the moment when her strength gradually deserted her, which eventually led her, for better or worse, to agree to be replaced at the stove by Mama, who eventually learned to make quite a number of her recipes, while continuing the series of her own, more elegant, desserts whose numbers increased with the years, since she enjoyed constantly expanding and increasing her repertoire beyond that of Romanian cuisine.

By the time she came to us, my mother later told me, Esti had perfectly mastered the art of creating, with a know-how and inspiration close to genius, a whole range of cakes and pastries that were clearly of Austrian influence, and that she must have learned in her native Transylvania. It was thanks to her presence that a permanent festival began of *fours secs* (**fursecuri**) (little cakes and biscuits that are not iced), creams, gâteaux and puddings of every shape and composition, There were **cornuleţe** (little horns), **corăbiele** (little boats), strudels and a whole range of delicious little pastries made with nuts, poppyseeds and raisins. She made extensive use of walnuts, especially for the Balkan-style baklava. Nor shall I ever forget her crisp **kadaif**, a very Turkish pastry, impregnated with heavy syrup and topped with whipped cream, and then the **cozonac**, a soft, yeast cake enriched with plenty of eggs, filled with walnuts for Christmas and sweetened curd cheese for Easter.

But that was not all. These pastries were supplemented by a plethora of various confections from the same family as Turkish delight, halva and **şerbet** which brought us the fragrance of the luxuriant, heady perfumes of the Orient that we felt to be so close to us.

At the time, when I was a child, these delicious sweetmeats and petits fours always stood in the cool shade on the large sideboard, filling elegant china baskets with wicker handles, as they awaited some unexpected guest, of the kind who would indeed frequently make an appearance. These visitors were of the type known as *musafir*, another expression that is clearly of Turkish origin. In my reveries, I pictured the sort of person who must have been this type of guest in previous centuries. They would have made their entrance, dressed in ample, gold-and-silk-embroidered caftans, their heads swathed in brilliantly coloured ornate turbans, in order to slowly savour those heavily sugared pastries; half-reclining on masses of embroidered silk cushions, they would draw voluptuous puffs on a nargileh as they sipped their coffee – Turkish of course – from tiny porcelain cups, too delicate for their thick fingers which were covered in huge rings.

But our *musafiri* were no longer attired in such accoutrements. Over time, they had acquired the appearance of some sort of uncle, a retired widower, a colleague of my mother's from the hospital, though most fell into the category of *tanti*, the title accorded to all those ladies who were cousins or friends of my mother. This is the term that was frequently used by a sector of the urban middle classes and in the country – meaning a sort of 'aunty'.

Whether or not they were blood relations, there was a host of *tantis*; I could create whole frescoes of these ladies, with their tics, their speech mannerisms, the stories of their lives and their characters. In short, the *tantis* occupied the foreground in the lives of many Romanian families.

The *tantis* or other *musafiri* would usually arrive without notice for a short visit on the stroke of five o'clock in the afternoon, surprising my mother just as she was waking from her habitual siesta. But she only pretended to be surprised, she was more or less expecting them, for this had become a custom. The *tantis* never arrived empty-handed, they always had a little gift under their arm, a modest offering, but generally something to eat; a sweetmeat, a delicacy of some kind, a pot of home-made jam, a basket of crystallised fruit, or a pot of *şerbet*, that thick, sugary paste, a speciality of Greek origin whose exquisitely delicate colours were provided by their natural flavours – raspberry, wild strawberry, lemon or chocolate. This was a much sought-after delicacy, a delicious and treasured delight, for its preparation required a special skill and stoical patience. Few people were actually capable of producing them but my Aunt Elena, who was Greek, was one of the few. She had married my Uncle Luca, a confirmed bachelor, at a time when he was over fifty. *Tanti* Elena was a tall woman with a matte skin, whose rather lifeless brown eyes were underlined by deep violet shadows. She was capable of continuously stirring her *şerbet* for hours on end until she obtained the desired consistency. This fastidious preparation made *şerbet* into something like the equivalent of caviar or foie gras, it would be fair to say. It was consumed in minute amounts, just a teaspoon filled with this exacerbated sweetness, a true concentrate of the most exquisite natural flavours. One would place it in a saucer next to a glass of ice water or plunge the teaspoon into the icy water and then take tiny sips while slowly sucking the rich paste to extract the whole essence of the exquisite taste of this confection.

A chapter about sweets could not possibly omit *dulceaţă,* another confection which the *musafir* would consume on the premises, unless one of the *tantis* herself brought a pot of it with her. Just like *şerbet, dulceaţă* was served on a little teaspoon placed on a saucer accompanied by the inevitable glass of cold water and often a demitasse of Turkish coffee. These preserves were of a different consistency and structure to those with which you are familiar. Mama would sometimes make them herself, with the expert collaboration of Esti, and this custom probably flourished in every home. The *tantis* vied with each other in their creations. These *dulceţuri* were not true jams for spreading, they were for serving almost exclusively to the *musafiri,* during an enjoyable gossiping session.

The *dulceţuri* were steeped in a syrup that was thick yet flowing and transparent. They were made from fruits in season that had to remain whole, an indispensable condition for a true *dulceaţă*; thus, apricots, cherries, plums as well as raspberries and wild strawberries floated in a heavy syrup, glistening in their jars with the lustre of precious stones. There were even some odder flavours, such as those made from green tomatoes, water-melon skins, green walnuts and that which I nicknamed 'the princess of preserves', the sublime rose-petal jam as well as the most elegant of them all, the black cherry preserve, made from those tiny bitter fruits that were dark maroon, almost black, in colour, which shone with a deep glow like that of pomegranate arils; the result was an astonishing flavour, rare, excessive, a mixture of bitter and sweet. I have never found such cherries elsewhere than in Romania.

When one of the *tantis* had made *dulceaţă*, she was quite proud of her achievement. Without false modesty, such a *tanti* would boast of her creation, victoriously brandishing the jar against the window so as to make its syrup, the precious, treacly, pale, amber-coloured liquid, glisten in the light. As an expert, she would praise the quality of the syrup, the intact shape of the fruits, proofs of exemplary success. Sometimes she would consent, a little unwillingly, to divulge her secret, for each of them had her own trick, her little knack.

The unrivalled champion of the raspberry or wild strawberry *dulceaţă*, however, was Lena-Tena. She was a frail creature, almost impossibly thin. With her washed-out blue eyes and very narrow face that trembled slightly, I had invented romantic tales about her that inflamed my imagination as a young girl; when she was young she had been a great beauty but her life had been ruined by an unhappy love affair to which she had dedicated the rest of her existence. She radiated great goodness and purity. For Lena-Tena I felt great tenderness combined with admiration, as if for the heroine of a romance, and I told myself that she had developed her great talent for making preserves to compensate for a lack of affection. Having had neither husband nor children, she found happiness in offering her magnificent jams to the children of others, to other families.

As soon as a *musafir* arrived, after the polite formalities, I would see Mama go to the kitchen, returning with a silver tray containing the saucer of *dulceaţă*, the glass of iced water and the cups of Turkish coffee, next to a steaming *ibric* (Turkish coffee-pot). That is how we would entertain a *musafir*.

For us, who lived at home, there was no question of us being allowed to gorge ourselves on these delights. In any case, they would be carefully locked away, for years at a time, in the most secret corner of the large sideboard. The only occasion on which we were allowed to taste them is when Mama or Esti used them to decorate their desserts, and even then they did so sparingly, so that we only rarely had the opportunity of actually tasting them 'in the same way as a *musafir*'.

And so I come to the simpler, everyday desserts, such as semolina or rice pudding, hot or cold, sprinkled with cinnamon or with the addition of a few fruits from a *dulceaţă*, adopting the role of 'the cherry on the cake'. Whether a pale golden apricot or a few fragrant raspberries, this addition lent a festive air to the most every-day dessert.

To finish a weekday meal sweetly, as was the rule, apart from the most frequently served rice and semolina puddings, Esti ingeniously varied the desserts as much as possible. Thus, from a whole series of puddings of a touching simplicity, her finest was *compot* which was nothing like the 'compôte' or stewed fruit of the English table. It might be described as a fruit soup since the fruits, which were kept whole, whether they were apples, pears, apricots, prunes or cherries, swam in a light syrup flavoured merely with a vanilla pod and lemon peel. Served very cold, this refreshing, light *compot* was very healthy and extremely welcome in summer, when the sun beat down relentlessly. Esti would also serve it any time we had an 'upset stomach'.

Without casting the slightest aspersion on the artistry that my mother devoted to the most elegant and elaborate desserts, 'in the French style', I now look back on those simple everyday puddings with a special affection and even a sort of tenderness. They inspire me differently, merely for their simplicity and modesty. I have just now caught myself thinking about those *clătite*, the forerunners of French crêpes. The same batter was used to make them but the shape given to 'Romanian pancakes' is different so that in my eyes they are a completely different dish. Instead of folding them in four as they do in Brittany, before covering them with a topping of choice, they were rolled up and served cold or hot. They were always sweet and filled either with *dulceaţă* or with chopped nuts and honey. In a more elaborate and very delicious version, the pancakes were then baked in the oven and garnished with a mixture of curd cheese, beaten eggs and raisins, the whole flavoured with rum and coated at the last moment with double cream.

That's what Romanian pancakes are like.

But the dessert that fills me with the most intense nostalgia, perhaps because I have not had the opportunity of tasting it since I left, is plum *găluşte*, a modest peasant dish. These are potato dumplings filled with plums, a humble, unostentatious dessert, the dessert of the poor, one that is almost monastic in its simplicity. Why do I seek my favourite dessert among those very sweets that are 'overlooked', on the margin, I have no idea. I can't even remember the recipe very clearly. As a simple pastime, at times when my morale is low, I merely need to leaf through my recipe books to find a little of that *joie de vivre* without which I am hardly myself. That is how I came to unearth this forgotten recipe for dumplings in an old cookery book, and Esti's recipe was probably not much different.

*

So this is the only series of actions that is needed in order to re-discover the traces of these amazing *găluşte*. Between the lines, I dig and delve into my memory, as if it were a picture book, trying to recall memories of Esti in the process of making them. I imagine her and I am thus able to bring her back to mind.

The recipe for găluşte – Plum Dumplings

You begin by boiling the potatoes in water. You then mash them adding an egg or two, a little flour and a pinch of salt. That is more or less the mixture in Romanian recipes. Esti would then knead this potato dough as thoroughly as she did everything else in order to obtain a firm consistency and a very smooth texture. She would roll it into a large ball which she would then divide into several pieces. She knew the lesson by heart.

I would pay close attention to these precise, almost mathematical, metamorphoses of the substance, and I noted how she would roll each piece into a long sausage-shape, each of which she would cut into little sections. She would roll each section between her palms into a round ball, a *găluşte*, the balls were slightly smaller than tennis balls. The time had come to fill them. With her index finger, Esti would press a stoned plum into each ball. The plums were the oval purple *zwetschken* plums or in winter she would use prunes that she had first soaked in water.

Meanwhile a large pot of water to which a pinch of salt had been added was simmering on the stove. As soon as it came to the boil, she would plunge the dumplings into it one by one, removing them with a slotted spoon as they came to the surface. When all had been removed from the boiling water, the *găluşte* would be deposited in a welcoming buttered dish and coated with a thick layer of breadcrumbs which had been moistened with melted butter, sugar and cinnamon. This same mixture would amply cover and flavour the soft, warm mass of dumplings. Esti would then dot them with a few shavings of butter before sliding the dish into a hot oven. I remember the way she had of delving into the fragrant mass with a big spoon to serve each of us a healthy portion of this dessert which was filling and nourishing. This feast of the poor...

Despite their simplicity, these plum dumplings still took quite a time to prepare. But there were also days for spontaneous sweets, the days on which Esti decided to improvise in mid-afternoon, on the spur of the moment, some 'surprise treats'. They were quickly made and quickly consumed and consisted of fat, round *gogoşi*, jam doughnuts – my favourites contained raspberry jam – or *minciunele* (the name means 'little lies'), crunchy pastries shaped like knotted ribbons or butterflies which she would fry in a large quantity of hot oil and which she would sprinkle while they were still hot with a cloud of icing sugar, and there were others...

When we were children, she would sometimes let us 'get involved' as it were, in making the cakes. We would 'help her' in the simplest operations, making it both a game and a method of learning to cook. We would crush nuts or knots strips of dough, then carefully transfer them to the pan of oil, taking care not to burn ourselves, all under the protective and vigilant eye of Esti. Or we would be set to stoning plums or cherries and using a pastry-cutter to cut the rolled-out dough into various shapes to make little biscuits in the shape of stars, half-moons or hearts. We were always proud of being allowed into the kitchen, that den of culinary delights, for a few brief moments.

If any remained from the previous day, most of these simple sweets would be transferred to the dining-room table where we got into the habit of keeping some permanently within reach, should any of us be seized with a craving when waking from the siesta, or we might have them as a dessert after dinner for one should never omit the final sweet touch to decently complete even the most frugal meal.

Esti never forgot to cover these remains with a napkin, especially in summer, so that they were protected from the dust and above all, to keep them from the flamboyant attacks of flies. This plague, a real national curse, would afflict us on a regular basis. The flies would reach the height of their insolence in the mid-summer heat when they seemed to triple in number.

And believe me, it was not easy, to get rid of the pestilent insects. We needed to act in concert, sometimes the whole family together, attacking them with increasing exasperation and an aggression that was close to hatred, armed with towels, fly-swatters and any improvised utensil that came to hand. We vied with each other as to who found the craftiest way of bringing them all down until there was not one left.

These exploits were soon forgotten as soon as we were able to relax, the little war having been won, in an innocent, peaceful siesta.

Christmas and New Year
Nineteenth letter to Agnes

A s the Christmas festivities approached, I suffered a sort of periodic crisis, the same feeling of subtle anguish, even irritation; yes, they always overcome me these holidays with their noise and fury, their avalanche of obligations and futilities. But finally, despite their invasive side, all their gormandising and excesses, they remain tender moments so that, all things considered, we wait for them to start again every year and when everything is over we are not unhappy. That's the way it will always be, there's nothing one can do…

So how did we Romanians celebrate the holidays? Here is a short description.

First of all, I must tell you that the term *reveillon* that the French use to mean Christmas Eve also exists in Romanian but we use it to refer to New Year's Eve. We pronounce it *révélyon* in our inimitable accent but for Romanians this event is not the night before Christmas, 24 December. Romanians attribute this neologism to the great pagan and secular feast of New Year. It is an adult festivity from which children are excluded, leaving the grown-ups, dressed in all their finery, in ball gowns and dinner jackets, the opportunity to enjoy themselves in a frenzy of unbridled merriment, dancing and drinking until dawn and eating food that was less traditional, less Romanian and rather more tinged with Western influence; these nights of joyous excess were abundantly watered, constellated more than ever with licentious pleasantries accompanied by the most sought-after and sophisticated foods. This was the general custom in Romania in the

1940s and 1950s; and more specifically, in my family, in Bucharest. For you, Agnes, who loves historical precision, I would situate the period that I will describe below as being somewhere between 1945 and 1955. I notice that it curiously concentrates my memories, no doubt because it was before the Great Collapse.

The festivities, which bore the authority and imprint of my mother's talent, began very late at night, at about eleven o'clock. To prepare for the event, the habitual siesta was considerably extended, followed by a dressing-up session because on such a night everyone, and especially the ladies, made a special effort with their attire. When the event was held in our house, and once all the guests had arrived, through the half-open door of our room where we were supposed to be asleep, my brother and I watched in our pyjamas, to glimpse fragments of the spectacle which we had so unjustly been denied. The swirling dresses, the great bursts of laughter, the rhythm of the music, we watched it all with fascination as if we were at the theatre.

A few years later, when I was finally old enough to come to the party, I shall never forget the first tango I danced with my father and my pride when, at the end of the dance, he kissed my hand, as was customary. I also had the right to join in that pudding-game consisting of a cheese *plăcintă* stuffed with notes called *răvaşe*. These notes contained amusing and naïve verses which were supposed to tell the fortune of the person who discovered them inside his/her portion of *plăcintă*, or sometimes they took the form of impudent verbal portraits in a few pithy verses which provoked sessions of collective laughter.

*

Christmas was another matter altogether, the atmosphere was completely different. Those Romanian Christmases arrived like a series of happy celebrations, family gatherings of a traditional nature, especially as far as the food was concerned, the abundance of which actually became synonymous with Christmas, this being the most propitious occasion for a competition in culinary prowess between every lady of the house.

The religious side was rather overshadowed, not to say forgotten, for few people in our circle attended midnight mass. I am still referring to my family and our close friends and relations, but I believe that our way of celebrating Christmas was the same everywhere, at least in the cities. In the country, I am sure that the situation was different. Perhaps that is the reason why the sort of Christmas Eve celebrations common among the pious in Europe did not happen here. So, like the English, our presents were not handed out on Christmas Eve but on the following day, 25 December, at lunchtime. French people find it strange but among Romanians, 24 December is just a prelude to the real festival and is completely quiet, though there is a subdued atmosphere of whispers, mysteries, comings-and-goings on tiptoe and secretly closing doors. The evening is dedicated to the decoration of the Christmas tree which is covered with beribboned and ornately wrapped presents. The parents were solely responsible for this, sheltered from the curiosity of the children who waited with bated breath, or at least pretended to do so, so as not to show that they were aware of the true situation, for instance, that last year Father Christmas had been played by none other than our Uncle Luca whose impeccably shined shoes would have been recognised by anyone, as they peeped from beneath the classic disguise of his long red cape. That's how I first discovered the truth behind the masquerade, due to this 'blunder'. Although for a long time thereafter I hypocritically pretended to be fooled.

Esti always referred to Uncle Luca, for whom she had a respect verging on idolatry, as *Domnu' Colonel*, that is to say 'Monsieur le Colonel' or 'the colonel'. He was my mother's older brother, a confirmed bachelor, who partied hard and loved pretty women, an almost professional skirt-chaser, it would seem. He nevertheless frightened us children due to his severe and imposing appearance and military bearing. Until he eventually married a Greek woman who was 'lodging' with us, he always lunched at our table, thus sharing with us the opportunity of tasting Esti's excellent cuisine.

These memories come tumbling in upon me. Romanian Christmases come back to me *en masse* and invade my thoughts like a huge coloured image, a succession of pictures as in a graphic novel, compact, rich, full of joyful opulence, endless, noisy banquets, a plethora of meals in succession that merge into one another, then separate and multiply in a deluge of gift-wrapped presents, laughter and song. With time, I have turned them into one huge Christmas, an all-embracing one covering those Christmases of plenty, those of my childhood as well as those of the subsequent times of austerity, and even the Christmases that I have spent here in France, among Romanians, for more than twenty years.

I again see that huge table laden with all sorts of traditional foods. It was the occasion bar none for the preparation of elaborate dishes that it would be impossible to serve every day. That is why the house was turned upside down for more than a week before Christmas. There wasn't just the food, the house had to be made ready so that guests could be received appropriately, so they could be cosseted and pampered, and we could all be seen at our best. For once, Mama and Esti shared the various tasks, culinary and household. Gusts of the most delicious smells emanated from the kitchen flooding the flat until the air became thick and unbreathable. It would have been unwise to open the windows because, even in Bucharest, it was bitterly cold. The cold hit us in the face and drew the luxury of lacy hoar-frost on our window panes in complicated and elaborate patterns. As if they were in an improvised playground, children amused themselves by blowing on the layer of frost, puffing out their cheeks to blow a hole in it so that they could see outside or scratching caricatures or letters to Father Christmas on it with their fingers.

First of all, the pig arrived from *Râmincu-Sărat*. I must have been very little because it was before my younger brother was born. This pig, whom we had visited during the summer holidays, had been carefully and tenderly fattened by my grandfather and *Miţa*, a distant relative and old maid who had always lived with my grandparents. I would compare her a little to Esti, for her devotion and the role she had acquired in the family.

I never knew my grandmother on my mother's side. I was only two years old when she died of diabetes. She was the valiant Dumitra, the Serbian, of whom my mother so often spoke. Perhaps as a result of her stories and photographs that I saw of her, I always

128

strongly felt her presence in the house at *Râmnicu-Sărat* that she apparently dominated with indisputable authority and just as much generosity that she radiated around her. As for grandfather, her husband, he was there, tall and straight as a pine tree, with that modesty and tenderness that he found hard to conceal under an exterior that was reserved, almost frigid.

During the summer holidays, we regularly stayed for long periods at *Râmnicu-Sărat*. It was a typically provincial small town in south-eastern Romania. Both my parents had been born there. We stayed in the same house in which my mother and her four brothers and sisters had lived and grown up. The old house was built in a traditionally Romanian style, consisting of a long frontage, flanked by a *pridvor*, an arcade supported on wooden columns. The bedrooms, which each bore the imprint of one of the members of the family, stood in a row, each leading into the other, and I tried to imagine each of their inhabitants with the atmosphere that would have prevailed there during their youth.

A series of open spaces, designed for various purposes and partitioned by wooden picket fences, surrounded the house. There was a courtyard, a kitchen-garden, a farmyard and a flower-garden in which my grandfather lovingly grew zinnias, large dahlias, snapdragons, and brightly coloured peonies. The garden also contained an old mulberry tree which we call *dud* in Romanian. And, God knows why, we waited every year for its little fruits to ripen, those juicy purple or white berries with which we loved to stuff ourselves but which had a rather musty, unpleasant flavour and left indelible purplish-black stains on our fingers and our tongues. The fruits of the dud may also have attracted us because each time we were forced to climb right up to the top of the tree to engage in acrobatic picking.

This *dud* had other functions that tested our daring and physical courage. Apart from its role as a food, the *dud* became a favourite nesting place for the chickens that were in the habit of spending the night safely in its dense foliage. One day, grandfather had the brilliant idea of attaching two ropes, linked by a plank, to one of its thickest branches. This swing became the focus of my favourite games. I would spend hours on it and every day I invented a thousand movements and daring manoeuvres in the company of Louly, daughter of Ion, the coachman. He had a permanent mission connected with our visits to *Râmnicu-Sărat*. He had to bring us, with our numerous suitcases, from the station and back to it again in his *trăsură*, the black, horse-drawn carriage that he handled with aplomb. The carriage had a *cornulețe*, a sort of hood that could be lowered or raised in case of rain or if the sun was too hot. It was the taxi of the period, in a convertible version.

We would return to Bucharest even more loaded down than before because each time we had been given provisions. A large basket contained fresh eggs, carefully individually wrapped in newspaper, a few local cheeses, fruits, juicy, fragrant tomatoes from my grandfather's kitchen-garden, a few flowers from his garden, dahlias and especially peonies. There was also honey from the hive owned by the neighbours opposite, the Stoilescus, whose daughter, Viorica, was also one of my playmates.

I imagined my mother, barely a teenager, gambolling in the huge courtyard dressed in her high lace-up boots and Peter Pan collars, just as she appeared in the sepia images that we would contemplate dreamily in the old photo album which grandfather, vanquished by our childish insistence, finally decided to extract from the old sideboard that was embalmed in the smell of coffee and the fragrant quinces that were kept in it. It was here, next to the tiny Turkish coffee cups, that the album, that precious object, was preserved. With slow, ceremonious gestures, after donning his narrow-rimmed glasses, grandfather would leaf through it for us with his large knobbly fingers, while answering the host of lively questions with the same reticence, since the album contained so many images, faces and scenes that excited our imagination.

*

But to return to the starting point, that is the Christmas pig. It was this famous pig which arrived from *Râmnicu-Sărat* where it had spent its days happily rooting in the farmyard, along with the geese and turkeys, or rather it was from the well-fattened flesh that all the good things came that we delighted in at Christmas. And here is proof of the inexhaustible vitality of the Romanian spirit: there was not just one Christmas feast but several. That is why we have always called 25 December, 'the first day of Christmas', followed by 26 December, 'the second day of Christmas' and finally the third. Each of the Christmas feasts was given in succession by a brother, a cousin or by grandparents and this distribution had been carefully arranged and passionately debated at least a month in advance. It did not happen without a certain amount of friction because, of course, each branch of the family claimed priority. For most of the mistresses of the house it was the highlight of the year, a grand occasion for showing off their culinary prowess and finally allowing their talents as a chef to blossom, hidden as they had been for the rest of the year in the humdrum chores of everyday life. So it became a contest to see who could present the finest *piftie*, the most melting *cozonac*, the most fragrant *caltaboș*, 'better than your cousin's, I promise you…', who would beat the record for the most delicious, succulent and melting *sarmale*. So you will understand why we needed at least three Christmas feasts – to find a way for all this talent and all this generosity to express itself. No point in adding that these records were then mercilessly judged at length for several weeks after the festival itself.

The copious repasts began, as is the custom with Romanian meals, at about three-thirty in the afternoon, sometimes even later but lasted until well into the evening, sometimes right into the night. Without a doubt, the central element in the meal, a totally oriental delicacy, was the *sarmale*. But this centrepiece had to be attained because it was preceded by a whole battalion of various pork dishes, which meant that certain less robust bellies were already full by the time the *sarmale* was served. That is how it was for me, at least, and for most children in general.

It was not until well after the *sarmale* that the *cozonac*, the king of desserts, made its appearance. That golden, meltingly rich yeast pastry, kneaded for so long with butter and several dozen eggs, flavoured with vanilla and lemon peel, took on various Christmas variations that Mama and Esti shared equally between them. All rivalry was banned for the occasion. In short, Esti reserved the walnut *co-zonac* for herself, while Mama had introduced a sort of dramatic licence, a sort of eccentric variation on tradition, in the shape of a chocolate *cozonac.*

So you see, I get indigestion just thinking about it. Too much, there was always too much at these Romanian Christmases. I shall stop now; but because you have insisted, you will hear the rest in another letter. There's too much to say, just as there was too much to eat.

More about Romanian Christmas
Twentieth letter to Agnes

I now realise that the most precious thing for me about Romanian Christmases was not so much the festival itself, the burst of joy on the palate and in the heart, but above all that long period of preliminaries, so full of mysteries and expectations, that preceded them. Ten days or so before the first day of Christmas, a dizzying combination of all sorts of fragrances and odours emanated from the kitchen and pervaded our nostrils, engulfing the house. There were sublimely delicious ones such as that of vanilla and raw eggs, produced by baking the *cozonac*; but curiously, there were others, stronger ones that could even be described as miasmas, nauseating smells whose effect was disconcerting especially as I never managed to work out exactly what caused them.

For a long time, I asked myself where these impossible, unbearable smells that always assailed our noses a few days before Christmas could have come from. What was their secret origin? It took me months to understand why on a specific date an unpleasant smell spread through the flat and that it actually came from the kitchen presided over by Esti. I learned eventually that it was, in fact, at those times that the various parts of the pig or turkey were being parboiled, an operation that was designed to contribute to that multitude of traditional dishes – sausages of all kinds, *caltaboş* or *piftie*, all those delights that were unavailable to use for the rest of the year.

When I discovered the reason, I found extra resources of courage to withstand these difficult tests, blocking my nose and even my ears, and telling myself 'one must take the rough with the smooth' and that probably applied to good food as well. Today, I realise that they also contributed, due to the effect of contrast, to expanding the range of odours that surrounded us, to heightening our sense of smell. It made us all the more appreciative of the good and pleasant odours, those that flattered our senses and God knows they were there in abundance.

Throughout this period of preparation, Mama and Esti fasted, moved by their simple and sincere faith, but without making a great fuss about it. At least one week before Christmas, they uncomplainingly suffered the restrictions of eating no eggs, no butter and no meat. But I don't think that the sacrifice was too heavy a burden because fast-day food, known as *de post*, by no means lacked flavour. In fact, Romanian cuisine contains a large number of delicious dishes that could be considered vegetarian, or even slimming, so much so that this short period of dietary restrictions was merely the most delectable possible variation on the seasonal menus. And we would happily consume these so called fasting or *de post* dishes for the rest of the year.

Nevertheless, on the very eve of Christmas, Esti and Mama would observe the 'black fast' (*post negru*), that is to say that they abstained from all food and only drank water. My father, who was less observant of the rituals, did not join them in this asceticism. As for us, we were spared these trials, with a single exception; we had no right to taste the egg-and-butter-enriched *cozonac* before Christmas Day, and any other dish based on butter and eggs was also proscribed. These minor restrictions merely stimulated our appetite and the wait seemed to us to be long and deeply painful. Watching dozens of different *cozonaci* of various sizes being paraded before our eyes, smelling their fragrance as Esti removed them hot from the oven, and seeing them lined them up in rows on the table, covered with clean cloths, was a form of torture.

It is due to these days of restrictions that, as soon as it was time, people literally threw themselves on the food. Believe me the wait was more than worth it, the meals that followed were so copious and succulent to excess that very few diners managed to stay the course on this real gastronomic endurance test. Tasting each of the dishes presented at the table was, for most people, an impossibility.

*

Christmas was, without a doubt, a family festival, and a food festival par excellence, an occasion on which all the various branches of the family could gather in outpourings of innocent joy. There reigned that atmosphere that was so Latin, so heart-warming, supplemented by all those delicious odours, the deafening noise of laughter and conversation that reached a crescendo towards mid-afternoon, gradually dying down at the end of the evening, due to fatigue caused by the effort of digestion and the excitement of the preceding days whose effect eventually made itself felt.

The children, far from being forgotten, occupied one of the most important roles and, believe me, there were plenty of presents which they rushed to discover at the foot of a real Christmas tree, lit by real candles, rather than the modern string of electric lights – a permanent danger that had caused a few small fires – but a custom that was absolutely essential. The tree sagged beneath a plethora of garlands and shiny baubles that our parents had used to decorate it the day before.

In a rather vague area of my memory, I still retain a few brightly coloured scenes, as if they were hand-coloured lithographs, of that old custom tinged with innocent piety, the Christmas carols celebrating the birth of Jesus which in Romanian are known as *colinde*[1]. A few days before Christmas – and the little fragments that I picture like these tuppence-coloured engravings must have happened when I was still a small child – groups of boy carol-singers known as *colindători* would go from door to door singing *colinde* and 'bringing the Good News'. One of them, usually the tallest, would carry a wand at the end of which hung a large coloured star made of crêpe paper, covered with shiny paper cut-outs of angels and the baby Jesus, produced from a whole range of popular imagery and also

1. See page 191 for a book about Romanian carols

135

evoking the Star seen by the Shepherds. They would sing *colinde*, those very traditional melodies in their clear, childish voices, beautiful songs that we ourselves would later sing together as we gathered round the Christmas tree on Christmas Day. We sang in the wavering light of the candles attached to the branches of the tree; my father would light the candles one by one just before handing out the presents.

It was customary to give the *colindători* nuts, apples and biscuits or a piece of *cozonac*. (*Ne daţi ori nu ne daţi?*). My mother would tell me how her brothers would themselves go out carol-singing with friends as *colindători* when she was a child. Unfortunately, this delightful tradition has ended, at least in the towns.

*

Guests arrived late for Christmas lunch, even later than the usual time for weekday lunches, sometimes even as late as four o'clock. We would kiss their cheeks, which were chilled and rosy from the cold outside, as they arrived, one by one, and they would tap the snow from their galoshes as they entered and make themselves comfortable.

This lateness was perfectly tolerated because the heavy snow made it even more difficult to travel. Christmas without snow was inconceivable. And we always had a heavy snowfall by Christmastime. In our best clothes and on our best behaviour, a little tense due to the excitement and eager to get to our presents, we patiently awaited the guests.

And finally, there was the first ring at the bell, and several of us would rush to open the door. We would jostle each other in the little entrance hall, in the narrow space between the mirror and the coat-stand. The gentlemen would remove the galoshes that all of us had to wear as protection from the slush, while the ladies replaced their rubber-heeled boots with elegant shoes that they had brought with them in a bag. These precautions were all the more necessary because people did a lot of walking in those days, private cars being almost non-existent at the time.

The dining-room was already redolent of the festivities. The table was laid, covered in the most beautiful damascene tablecloth and the best tableware which my mother had brought out for the occasion. More than ever, Esti reigned as queen of the kitchen on that day and she bustled about adding the final touches, an olive here, a pickled gherkin there, or re-folding a napkin; meanwhile, my father would be placing little name-cards in front of each plate adding to the names of the diners his own humorous caricatures, alluding to the various quirks that each possessed.

First came the *gustări*, a succession of little hors d'oeuvres comparable to Spanish tapas; the little dishes on the table would include *telemea* – ewe's milk cheese – tiny little *chiftele*, pearl onions, olives and a few pickled gherkins. A tiny glass or two of *ţuică* warmed the guests' stomachs. There immediately followed a whole series of pork dishes and various cooked meats, all of them homemade, including the succulent *caltaboş*, a rather heavy, greasy white pudding made from pork offal and rice, as well as *piftie*, a chaud-froid of pigs' ears and feet, heavily laced with garlic, two thin soups containing horseradish, and as condiments there were English mustard and cucumbers in brine, all accompanied by a steaming hot *mămăligă*.

This part of the meal was 'not my cup of tea'. When I was little, I did not like the gelatinous consistency of the *piftie*, nor the *caltaboş*, a fat sausage whose soft, greasy texture disgusted me. I decided that these were dishes 'for grown-ups'; needless to say, I now hunger after them because they are specialities that are difficult to make and hard to find. As a child, I did not have much of an appetite and a few slices of cured meat, a piece of salami and one or two salads were enough for me. Moreover, what with the overexcitement of the preparations and the waiting, the mere sight of the heavily laden table was enough to take my appetite away.

But that is true of all children who are so stuffed to the gills after the hors d'oeuvre that they cannot eat another morsel. There was nothing to be done about it, I never managed to taste the cold turkey presented on a bed of green salad decorated with tiny gherkins and olives, nor the 'beef salad' and even less the divine *sarmale* that steamed next to a huge mound of *mămăligă*. From this series of meals, all I retained for a long time was the symbolic meaning and a sense of frustration which fortunately I was able to make up for amply in later years.

*

The *sarmale* were the true *pièce de resistance* of the Christmas feast and they are also considered to be our national dish. They consist of whole cabbage leaves pickled in brine wrapped around small, well-seasoned packages of stuffing. The *sarmale* are simmered for hours in a rich sauce containing white wine, herbs and spices as well as a few strips of smoked bacon, and this combines wonderfully with *mămăligă*. This is *mămăligă's* true calling and for the occasion, the dish was even more steaming, luscious, golden and well-cooked, presented as a firm, shapely ball. This great Christmas *mămăligă* had to be sufficient to feed at least twelve people, or even as many as two dozen, a number of guests that was by no means unusual at Christmastime.

The process of making *sarmale* was long and complicated and it was a task rarely embarked upon at other times of the year. In any case, it was difficult to eat them too often, it's as if you were given the same rich food to eat every day of the week. Placed at the heart of this huge and special feast, they were themselves quite a feat to digest. Even the greediest of guests found themselves unable to manage them when the moment finally came. It was up to the hostess, in this case my mother, to put all her diplomacy to work to coax each diner into accepting the largest number of *sarmale*, for better or worse.

'Come along, let me give you just one more you'll see how good it tastes…'. This was a sort of sentimental blackmail because it was a point of honour to be able to make the best *sarmale* and everyone tried to do their best to honour the mistress of the house.

It was now that the men came into their own, the 'real' men because Romanians are rather macho, and there were those who, come hell or high water, were not afraid to accept a dozen or so, finally

138

managing to put away twenty or even thirty *sarmale*. They even vied with each other for the record. I have seen one of them swallowing no fewer than forty *sarmale* under the admiring gaze of his fellow diners. His name was Mircea Bogdan, may God rest his soul, a sort of monument to Bucharest gastronomy, who is now long dead. He had a massive but rounded build, though without being flabby, pale and obese, his skin clear and matte, and it was a real treat to watch him eat. He was the embodiment of praise for the foods of the earth, a really Rabelaisian figure.

These sorts of men, those of exceptional machismo, loved to display their talents whenever they considered the moment was right by accompanying the *sarmale* with one or two green chilli peppers of the type that cause unbearable burning in the mouth. The ladies found this feat particularly impressive. Needless to say, numerous glasses of wine or *ţuică* were consumed to wash down this Gargantuan feast.

Yet most people quailed when it was finally time for the *sarmale*. We children always asked permission to leave the table well before the *sarmale*, to play hide-and-seek among the piles of coats, galoshes, living-room chairs and the used dishes. It was only when the dessert appeared that our appetites miraculously returned and we rushed back to the table.

A few ladies simperingly agreed to be served one of two *sarmale* 'just for a taste'. Sometimes they did so surreptitiously, merely to judge the skill of the cook and compare the result with their own handiwork, and this was done in a highly critical spirit, quite devoid of any leniency or compassion.

It should be said that none of the leftovers of the meal were wasted, since the huge pot containing the divine *sarmale* was placed in the oven the next day, and some were consumed as much as a week later, which made them taste even more scrumptious and succulent, as they had had time to be covered with a light brown crust, which became ever more caramelised, as the cooking liquid reduced and concentrated into the purest essence of their aroma. That is how the connoisseurs preferred them. 'Leftover *sarmale*' were at the absolute finest.

After spending many hours at table, it was finally time for the dessert, time for *cozonac*, the Christmas dessert, in all its splendour, the *cozonac*, a relative of the brioche, which Esti's powerful white arms had kneaded with passion and vigour for almost a whole night. The result was a dough of the utmost airiness, meltingly light and flavoured as appropriate with vanilla and grated lemon rind. There was a plain variety and another that was dotted with raisins and yet another kind filled with a mixture of well-sugared ground walnuts.

No one was in a hurry to come to the end of this meal which seemed interminable. Having begun so late, it extended late into the evening. The guests took their time. The abundance of drink made it possible to digest the rich food and loosened tongues, triggering an atmosphere of chatter, laughter, joy and even song.

There was *ţuică* of course, served ice-cold in tiny glasses, but most people preferred wine, the wine that came in a demijohn, *damigeana* in Romanian, which my father and my uncle Gicu, my mother's younger brother, would go and fetch directly from the wine-makers, who were peasants living on the outskirts of Bucharest. Wine bought from shops was too expensive and generally from 'under the counter'. The wine of which the guests amply availed themselves may not have been a great wine but it must have been very drinkable and thanks to this wine, the atmosphere became so warm that often, shortly after the *sarmale,* the flat resonated to the sound of drinking songs, the whole table singing them together, unabashedly and effortlessly. It only needed one guest to set the rest off, someone 'with a voice' such as Uncle Teodor, a bass, who would start with an old Romanian ballad such as '*Îţi mai aduci aminte, Doamnă*...' Do you remember, Madam, it was late and autumn was here already', or '*Paşte, murgule, iarbă verde*' (Go and graze, my handsome brindle horse, on the green grass in the meadow'). Aunt Lala, who was rather saucy and a little coquettish, would 'take the bit between her teeth' and bring the table to life with another of these drinking songs, of which she knew all the words, and everyone would join in for the chorus.

When night fell, after Turkish coffee, the guests were finally overcome by fatigue. Heavier, replete, but happy, they finally decided to go home, one after the other, though not without first showering the most lavish compliments on the mistress of the house.

The distribution of the presents had happened at the start, before the meal began, while thinking was still clear. Everyone stood around the tree and we sang *O brad frumos* which is 'O Christmas Tree' in Romanian, or other Romanian Christmas songs and fragments of *colinde*. It was inconceivable not to sing such songs for Christmas.

The children were often terrorised by a sort of sentimental blackmail which consisted in not handing over the present before the child had performed their party piece, consisting of a nursery rhyme, a little song or a poem to Father Christmas. It had taken the children several weeks to learn their piece, yet memory lapses often occurred at the last moment due to the excitement.

Very little seems to have changed since then. I don't think that Romanian Christmas is very different from other Christmases anywhere else and at other times. Here in Paris, all that is lacking is the deep snow and the frost covering the windows.

*

I have never enjoyed noisy celebrations. On these occasions where one has the impression that one is being forced to enjoy oneself, I feel as if I am being dragged down despite myself into an inevitable maelstrom. That is how I have always felt in the midst of an event that is too rowdy, excessive, I feel I am suffocating from the smoke and the smell of food. Thus, when I was on the verge of adolescence, I got into the habit of removing myself to some deserted balcony, and staying there in the dark. Overcome by a sort of inexplicable sadness, I would escape from the crowd. I felt the need to breathe fresh air and look at the stars, if only for a few moments. Then I would return to the festivities as if it were an obligation.

And now, perhaps from the effects of age, during the winter holidays, I run away and hide. I try to eschew as far as possible their more tiresome aspect, the rhythm of ritual obligations and gestures which exasperates me more than ever. I prefer to leave Paris and spend Christmas and the New Year far from the city, in the country, somewhere peaceful. It is there that I can better see and sense the wild life, the cold, the earth, the trees and the sky, and the simplest foods take on another aspect. I am moved by the simplicity of a piece of bread beside a lamb chop grilled in the hearth under a layer of thyme and coarse salt, the fragrance of which seems to me unique and precious, and I tell myself that this is where my happiness lies. That is how I seem to rediscover the real extent of my martyred, delinquent senses. My unstable, proven sensitivity retraces itself, in a way that is more withdrawn and more conscious, but gradually my heart grows lighter and the Christmas festivities I enjoy, far from seeming austere, regain their original meaning and a joy that is truer.

De Post – Lenten austerity and abstinence
Twenty-first letter to Agnes

With my wooden spoon, I stir and toss and mix from time to time the onions that are turning golden in the frying-pan, they slowly brown as I lovingly watch over them. I am impregnated with the persistent and uncouth odour of fried onions, which I always savour. For perhaps the thousandth time, I am making *fasole bătută*. This time it is because it is the day before Easter and this purée of haricot beans with fried onions easily slips into the menu for Lent or *de post* as it is known in Romanian.

Between stirrings, I twirl around in my kitchen, I pirouette in a whirlwind, wandering from one utensil to the next, in an attempt to make three dishes simultaneously.

Like Esti's kitchen in Bucharest, my kitchen is small and over-crowded. It's always the same scenario: I keep bumping into the same sharp corner of a cupboard door that yet again I have forgotten to close. 'Miss Daydreamer', my mother used to call me. Mine is far from being the 'laboratory-kitchen' with its cold, clinical atmosphere. It's a mess. The chequered cloth is now too wet to be useful for wiping. But I enjoy working in this chaos, it's mine. I work a little like my mother did, conscious of being one of those active, occupied, busy women who try to do it all, family, work, cooking, while preserving an undamaged passion, a joy, a pleasure, come what may.

Since both my hands are full and sticky with traces of flour, I open the refrigerator with an elbow. A little dried *mămăligă* is burning somewhere. A glass slips and shatters into pieces, I push the debris with my foot, never mind, I'll sweep it up later. And can you believe it? In this crazy atmosphere, I am in my seventh heaven.

As soon as the onions are properly fried, well browned, they will be added to the haricot bean purée whose fragrance is already pervading the kitchen with its heady perfume, the result of the addition of so many garlic cloves. I feel my hands to be deliciously impregnated with this odour of garlic and raw onion, and the smell will linger for a long time, I know. The handle of the wooden spoon also bears the intimate mark of various smells. It is stained and has burn marks, and I love it. This pathetic object could almost be read like a dictionary of gastronomy.

No, my dear, my kitchen has nothing of that purified, clean, photogenic, intellectual setting of brand new, modern kitchens, those that are purchased by mail order or that can be admired in the display windows of department stores. Here it is the precarious that predominates, there are lots of falls and breakages and items are crushed; there are shards of glass in the corners, the walls are thickly coated with the glaze of accumulated vapours and I am sorry to say that the sink is as full of dirty dishes as a bus is full of passengers during rush hour. My kitchen is a crucible of love, a furnace, a field of battle, and the flavour of the dishes that emerge from it is itself different. Their birth is governed by nothing more than intuition, instinct, pleasure. I would call it a sensitive, poetic cuisine.

Easter, I am telling you, is for later; our Orthodox Easters are the most important, the most sacred and the most joyous festival of the year. This is the feast of light and spring. In order to prepare for it, I insist on following the custom, to keep these days *de post*, just as my mother and Esti did. For a week I shall live on nothing but vegetables, grains and vegetable oil. Will I have the courage to keep the last day of black '*post*', as my mother did, a day of complete fasting?

During these Lenten days, these days *de post*, a beneficial dietetic calm prevailed which felt as if it were really needed. The gorging topped, it was a time of purification, one almost became addicted to this abstinence with a modicum of pride in this victory over oneself. It was an opportunity to reinvent daily habits, to take time out to experience that 'other taste' produced by a number of dishes that were no less succulent and delectable but that one tended to forget during the test of the year. Mama had great affection for these dishes which she would also make for us at times other than festivals, especially on Fridays which she always considered to be fast days, *de post*. She had inherited these recipes from her own mother, who made these dishes in *Râmnicu-Sărat*, during her childhood. The recipes must be very old, she would confide in us, such as for example those fruit stews of apples, apricots, quinces or prunes, and many more.

In principle, fish was supposed to be the basis of a Lenten meal, but since fish was virtually unobtainable in the market, it was replaced by vegetables, cereals and an abundance of spices which not only made them edible but turned them into delicious dishes that could hardly be called austere. Of course, there were a number of green soups, herb soups, which I have already mentioned. I would like to quote you two of my favourite recipes, those marvels of simplicity that I love to make here, in France, throughout the year. It's an easy paradox to explain, that is how Lenten dishes can be transformed into veritable sins of gluttony.

Let me tell you here about the leeks with olives and the courgette *pilaf*. Both are served hot or warm. To my knowledge, there is no more irresistible and thus more hypocritical way of bridging the gap until the Great Easter Feast, that night when all the barriers are taken down and every kind of food is permitted once again.

*

Leeks with Olives

Slice up the whole of each leek, merely discarding the toughest of the green parts and the roots. Fry the leek in oil, sprinkle it with a tablespoon of flour, mix well with a wooden spoon, and stew until lightly coloured. Separately, add a little hot water to a can of tomato purée and add this to the leeks. Sprinkle with a few herbs, especially parsley, a few celery leaves, and leave simmer. Add more hot water if necessary. A few minutes before the end of the cooking time, boil up a handful of pitted black olives, rinse them under the cold tap, drain them and sprinkle them over the leeks. Serve warm or even cold; the dish will keep until the next day, or even for several days.

*

Recipe for Courgette Pilaf
Pilaf de dovlecei

Heat some oil and let the rice 'flower' in it, that is to say, wait until the grains of rice turn white and swell slightly. Then add one or two chopped onions and cook with the rice; peel the courgettes and slice them into rounds then into little dice and add them to the pan. Cook everything for a few minutes, stirring with a wooden spoon. Cover with warm water, three times the volume of the rice. Season with salt and pepper and continue to cook. When ready, sprinkle copiously with chopped dill. Depending on taste, this dish may be served hot or cold. When not prepared during periods of fasting, it can be used to accompany a meat dish but, in my opinion, this vegetarian *pilaf* is even more delicious when served warm as an hors d'oeuvre.

Turkish coffee time
Twenty-second letter to Agnes

> '...*According to an ancient tradition, coffee was discovered by a shepherd who noticed that his flock was especially lively and hilarious whenever it had grazed on the berries of the coffee-bush.*'
> (Brillat-Savarin, *The Physiology of Taste*)

When visiting me, you have often tasted this typical beverage that you had sipped in Greece, where it is forbidden to call it anything but 'Greek coffee'; and you have done so in Turkey, where it received its true name, or again among the Lebanese who flavour it with cardamon seeds.

As a convinced patriot, but especially so as to explain the subtleties of taste, the differences, I must repeat that Turkish coffee made in the Romanian style is not at all the same thing.

What gives the universal meaning to this totally oriental custom is the whole atmosphere that surrounds it since, for Romanians, and no doubt for the other peoples who are addicted to it, Turkish coffee is a true ritual and its role, which is by no means a commonplace one, places it above being a mere drink. It is the equivalent of dotting the 'i's in a text, it serves, in fact, to punctuate, to divide time, to highlight, to enhance, the various moments of the day. Its presence, which is almost intangible, even spiritual, I would say, although imbued with sensuality, is indispensable to us.

I have sometimes confided in you, you will remember, a few little anecdotes associating Turkish coffee with the *musafiri*, those impromptu visitors who linger by a house as soon as they can smell the heady perfume of Turkish coffee. When I think about it, so synonymous with comfort, relaxation, well-being, sensuality, that dense, warm fragrance seems to rise immediately in my nostrils. The aroma of the coffee beans that are roasted at home, or the fragrance that titillated our nostrils everyday at specific times, when my mother prepared it. As the heiress to these almost ancestral customs which she claimed, like so many other recipes, to have learned from her mother, Mama turned it into a veritable rite in our home in Bucharest, at which she officiated like no one else. The authority she had acquired had caused her to win the exclusive right to perform this task. That is how the slightest gesture in the preparation of Turkish coffee by mother remains imprinted forever on the sensitive support for this sensory memory whose importance and infinite richness I have come to appreciate with time.

For Mama, the coffee ritual – for that is how I like to describe it – was associated with very specific times of day, those 'coffee moments', the pretext for long, chatty conversations of which she was in such need and which enabled her to express her generous heart and extrovert nature.

I remember her at the time when I was beginning my career as an artist. At about four-thirty in the afternoon, I would hear her knocking on the door of my improvised studio in one of the bedrooms, gently 'so as not to disturb you'; she would ask me every time 'whether I didn't feel like a *cafeluţă* – a little coffee – although she knew the reply in advance. And she would then slip into the room bearing her little paraphernalia. On a silver-plated tray, she would place the *ibric*, the receptacle from which there escaped that emanation that was subtler than any other, warming, intimate, even intoxicating; there were also two elegant little porcelain cups, sitting on their saucers. Then, as soon as she had filled the cups with that delicacy of gesture that demonstrated all the importance and tenderness that she devoted to this familiar ritual, she would install herself comfortably in an armchair and begin to take little sips of the coffee while commenting on its quality, 'Today, I made it well' or 'It was better yesterday, don't you think?' or, 'I have sweetened it too much'.

This ritual and the pleasure that she took from it began for her with the preliminaries. For there was a whole procedure and each of the stages had its own importance. She had usually ground the coffee beans well in advance. At one time, she would even roast the green beans herself, in a little saucepan that had become blackened from use. That exciting perfume went straight to our heads. Then, to mill it, she would use her old brass Turkish coffee mill. This was a handsome object, cylindrical in shape, covered in lovely, carefully engraved geometrical patterns. I still preserve this relic, and for me it is filled with a whole history of odours and gestures. I don't use it any more but sometimes I take it out to revive the contact with my hands, I touch it, I caress it, this metal that seems to vibrate under my fingers.

I can still hear my mother's words: 'The taste of good coffee', she would often say, 'begins with the quality of the grind, which must be performed very precisely for the specific purpose of making Turkish coffee'.

All these subtleties are difficult to obtain with an electric coffee-grinder. That is why, here in Paris, it is better to buy it, ready-made, from a coffee-roaster's, where one can request 'a Turkish grind'. This means that the beans must be much more finely ground than usual. Once again, one pays the price of modernity because, apparently, in exchange for this improvement in convenience, some of the charm and poetry has been excised from the ritual.

So, our Turkish coffee began with grinding the beans. While she wedged the cylindrical mill between her knees, Mama would start to talk, while constantly turning the handle. Later, when my mother had aged, it was my brother who took on this task since it required a certain strength in the wrist. This is her recipe, which I got from her, and it is easy to make, quite simple. It may not be identical to that used in other Romanian families or in other countries in which Turkish coffee is drunk.

First of all, to make real Turkish coffee, it is essential to use the traditional vessel known as an *ibric*. It is made of copper or enamelled metal and is trapezoid in shape, being very narrow at the top and widening out below. It has a long handle, a very functional extension to avoid burning one's hand. My mother even used a special spoon with a long, thin handle, to be able to stir deep down in the *ibric* with complete safety.

Turkish coffee is pre-sweetened. Sometimes, out of politeness one asks guests how heavily sweetened they would like it. True Turkish coffee is drunk very sweet. A little coffee cup is used as a measure; one sugar lump or a teaspoon of sugar should be used for each teaspoon of coffee ground 'Turkish-style', per cup of water.

One begins by filling the *ibric* with water, while adding corresponding measures of sugar; my mother would only add the coffee when the water came to the boil. This is when you need to be able to move quickly. At the very moment the water begins to boil, the *ibric* is swiftly removed from the fire so that it does not boil over and the measures of coffee are added while stirring well with the spoon. The *ibric* is then replaced on the fire, only for it to be removed again as soon as the water returns to the boil. This little manoeuvre is repeated once more and that's all there is to it. Here is a trick that will come in handy if you don't like tasting the grounds: before starting to pour the coffee, sprinkle the contents of the *ibric* with a few drops of cold water and this will allow the grounds to settle. It also stops the Turkish coffee from becoming too thick and sticking unpleasantly to the lips, the kind that is sometimes served in so-called 'ethnic' restaurants.

Let the coffee rest for a few moments so that there is time for the grounds to settle completely. It is customary not to throw away the foam that forms on the surface and which in Romanian is called *caimac*. In fact, one begins by delicately taking a little of this *caimac* and adding it to the bottom of each cup before pouring in the coffee.

Afternoon Turkish coffee was not the only time dedicated to the partaking of this subtle elixir. It was also welcome at the end of heavy meals, though never in the evening as it prevented sleep, nor again after lunch in order to maintain the effectiveness of the siesta that followed. Its essential role was always linked to that moment in the afternoon when one takes greater pleasure in tasting it, to wake thoroughly out of the siesta, before launching oneself into other activities.

Speaking of Turkish coffee, one cannot help but mentioning that charming custom, half-superstition, half-amusement, of 'reading' the future in coffee grounds. In fact, after having drunk their coffee, many Romanians, especially women, automatically turn their coffee cup upside down so that the grounds flow into the saucer. The grounds should not be too thick nor too liquid and it is important to swirl the cup lightly so that a thin layer of grounds covers the interior like delicate lacework. That is why the cup has to be white and, if possible, of porcelain.

After a few moments, the grounds, having had the time to dry out, form a sort of lacy pattern in which elaborate forms, haphazard designs, signs of destiny, predictions can be discerned and interpreted. More by intuition and playfulness than by learning the few simple rules that can be combined with a little imagination and humour. I have known women in Romania who managed to achieve a certain reputation for their gifts as 'coffee grounds clairvoyants' and people beat a path to their door in order to consult them.

In short, an enchanting air of magic always surrounds Turkish coffee. Yes, that is how I would describe that very special sentiment, which is more than just a feeling. I won't say any more, except that I already feel pervaded by the exciting fragrance of the coffee, whose heady perfume makes my head spin.

Like a Vermeer painting
Twenty-third letter to Agnes

Working with the hands, even on the most humble and everyday tasks, has something noble about it in that it allows the mind to wander freely as if to liberate one from a rebarbative gesture that is insignificant in itself. Often when I devote myself to one of those inevitable household chores, such as ironing or washing up, my mind wanders and I allow myself to be invaded by images, memories. I embroider and cobble together fragments of thought or let them float along as they choose.

In the kitchen, I stand in front of the open window over the sink; I am washing dishes, absorbed in the banality of this daily grind. Having to be sure to perform the task thoroughly, I get down to it. I observe my hands, plunged in the sink, slowly applying themselves to this tedious operation, so that I even forget who it is that is standing in front of the window doing the work, I no longer know if it is me or someone else. My gaze wanders as usual over the impersonal, immobile and dull view of the buildings opposite, sun-bleached, scraped and eroded by rain, as if they had been calcinated in some ravaging fire. Dreary windows, open or closed, regular or misshapen, arranged haphazardly over the frontages by a fleeting hand. A curtain here, a brightly coloured cloth there drying in the air, a plant that clings tenaciously to the wall.

Suddenly, like a strident cry, there is an exception to this grey monotony – an event! There, over there, in the distance, bang – with an explosive burst, the lemon-yellow shutter of a flamboyant new building, underlined by a strip of blue sky. That shutter has been winking at me for ages. We understand each other. Depending on the day, it may be half-open, completely closed, morose, or when the time is at its most melancholy, it is slightly concealed. A ray of sunshine sometimes bring it alive, a darkened sky will blot it out and it is left to merge into the landscape.

As for me, I watch these little changes, their imperceptible music. I simply try 'to be there for it'. It's a difficult task. My gaze follows the back of the walls, the splashes of colour, a piece of string hanging down, a beam that stands out from the rest by its solidity. And over all, the benediction of a vast sky that is always made of light, which predominates and sometimes allows its sharp image to be reflected on a receptive wall tile.

*

For a long time, I tried to concentrate on finding these 'washing-up moments', the echo of similar moments, a long time ago. They were as alike as twins. Yes, I can see it now. It is not me, it is Esti, sprinkled with the light of dusk, who is doing the washing up as if she were performing some ancient ritual. And in fact, she also used to stand in front of the kitchen window, in Bucharest. It was such a long time long ago.

Could I have invented, dreamed this counterpoint image, that mythical moment?

At home in Bucharest, Esti's kitchen window also looked out over roofs with, in the foreground, the greyness of a row of walls. At the back of the building in which we lived there were two openings, the little balcony that opened off the dining-room which was known as the 'back balcony' and which was also used to some extent for storage, so it was cluttered with bottles, soda siphons and old pots. The other was Esti's kitchen window from which there was a view of the neighbouring houses and down below, the little service courtyard. Then, at the opposite end of the flat, there was the 'front balcony' which projected further; it was very long, less dark and it overlooked the street and the facades of the houses on the other side of the street.

From the back balcony one could glimpse far down below, as if at the bottom of a deep well, the little interior courtyard. Just below the balcony there was a down-pipe which I remember as a sort of bluish-black hole, protected by a black grille, from which rats would sometimes emerge. As a child, I would contemplate them with a mixture of horror and fascination. Next to this, in the little courtyard, the concierge could often be seen cursorily sweeping, as if nothing had happened, while humming some popular tune or exchanging comments with Esti, who was leaning out of the kitchen window, about the weather, rising prices or some other local gossip.

From here in the kitchen, if one raised one's eyes slightly and looked straight ahead, beyond the row of chimney-pots on the closest buildings, one could see fragments of buildings exhibiting their oddly-shaped corners and medley of colours, and one would glimpse, as if it were in another world, one of those open-air restaurants where people would go in the evening to dance to a local band and eat delicious grilled meat. There were masses of such establishments in Bucharest, they are places that I miss so much now, these *grădina de vară* as they are known in Romanian. This particular one had the evocative name of *Doru'Ancuţei* which means 'Nostalgia for *Ancuţa*'. The window was Esti's 'observation post' as well as ours, as children, for she would often call us over to join her at this place of contemplation which was so utterly magical.

The spectacle, being both far and near, bewitched us. In some measure it was Esti's 'television screen' before that form of technology had entered our homes. It was also an 'outing' for her, especially from the time she decided not to venture downstairs any more.

At the end of the day, as soon as the band struck up the first foxtrot, she would install herself comfortably at the window, elbows on the table, as if in a box at the theatre. And she watched, enthralled. She breathed in the air of festivity, the strains of light music, consisting of a medley of hackneyed old favourites. Delighting in this with her, we gorged ourselves on the spectacle of the couples entwined who twirled in that splash of rather dim light but which seemed to us to be utterly brilliant.

Up above, the stars twinkled softly and seemed to be continuing the festivities in the skies, up to which there rose the faint but exciting odour of grilled meat. This was the aroma of the *mititei*. Esti thus identified with pleasures she had never known even for a fleeting moment. Meekly marvelling, she allowed herself to be captivated by the sparkle of this circle of light, teeming with life, and it made her happy.

During the sessions to which she treated herself almost every evening, she would spot the most imperceptible changes, subtle alterations. Sometimes the festivities stopped for a few days, or even for weeks, for some unknown reason. Then Esti was disappointed, almost wistful. And when they started up again, resplendently, it was like a première at the opera.

Then, one day, this theatre of fortune ceased to exist for good. Just like that, it disappeared. Like so many other things, without a word of warning. Esti was distraught, she even shed a few tears, but recovered as usual and was back to her old self. There were other things she could rely on. And henceforward, her headquarters, her observation post, moved to the other side of the flat which was her whole universe at the time, to the larger and better kept balcony, the 'front balcony' from which she could watch the street.

At a later stage, Mama discovered that she had green fingers and planted geraniums, tulips and zinnias in window-boxes. So, in the late afternoon, Esti would sit there, among the flowers, in her new sentry-box from which she would observe the passers-by, the street-vendors, the barrel organ-grinder with his parrot who did his usual round. The house opposite was occupied by Mr. Popa and his family. He had once owned a bistro on the ground floor of our building but it was confiscated, as were all privately-owned businesses. The site had since become neglected and visibly declined and one could see drunkards staggering out of the run-down café from which there escaped a heavy odour of plonk. Esti had much to say about this development, and her pointed remarks had a freshness and humour that always delighted us.

Esti would keep watch on the balcony, with our dog, a basset hound named Kafka, beside her; they both seemed to be on the same wavelength, plunged into a sort of meditation, at a time of candour, innocence and a certain manner of being in harmony with things, with the universe.

The City Mouse and The Country Mouse
Twenty-fourth letter to Agnes

This evening, on my way home, I gave myself a little treat, I bought a pot of honey. You are familiar with the spectacular flavour of this food of the gods which I love to taste on its own. I bought it from the man who comes over every Saturday and sets out his little stall on the pavement of the rue de Lévis. He unfolds a small table on which he arranges a pyramid of pots of honey of various sizes, announcing their origin and their flavour by means of hand-written labels. Around them, he sets a number of other products from the same family: whole fragments of pale yellow honeycomb, pollen for beauty care and to maintain youthfulness; for children, there is honey cake, *pain d'épices*, bearing the label 'guaranteed genuine'; and even those soft slices of nougat which in Romania we call *halviţă*, which I vaguely remember, as if through a fog or from a distance, from my early childhood. I put a morsel in my mouth, the taste is delicious, melting, but the substance has an uncomfortable habit of sticking to my teeth; I try and dislodge it, become irritated, and finally tell myself I won't eat it any more despite its delightful taste.

Before opening the pot of honey, out of pure gluttony, I hold the pot up to the light to gaze at the consistency and depth of the transparent, amber honey, and I delay for as long as possible the luxurious, long-awaited moment when I can taste it. It is that same honey, yes, the same substance, the same colour and the same matter that I would rediscover with delight in the early morning, as I leapt from my bed, when I used to spend weeks at a time in Dobriceni in the summer.

With half-closed eyes, I feel with my hands and find the edge of the barrel filled to the brim with honey which stood at just the right place, as a sort of night table. So within arm's reach, upon waking, I always had a ladle that I could use to dip whenever I felt like it into that darkness impregnated with the heavy scent of honey, in order to draw out bowlfuls of the precious amber.

Very cold water helped this beneficent substance to better slide down my throat. It is the custom of the region. This honey had been collected from the bees belonging to the priest who tended his hives like a poet. He would talk to the bees, whispering tenderly in their ears, he would approach them without protection, his hands and face uncovered, and was never stung. They trusted him.

I had discovered this little village in Oltenia, in southern Romania, and I would go to stay there regularly for long periods. That is where, for the first time, I felt those peasant atavisms become resurgent in my veins. Thus, young and newly married at the age of seventeen, I, the painter, the woman from Bucharest, the 'young lady' from the city, finally experienced true country life which to my great joy enabled me to discover another image of Romania. For me, this was a beneficial change of scene, I delighted in it with a sort of exalted fervour.

I lived in the village with a family of notables, my parents-in-law. My father-in-law was the village priest, and what's more, a bee-keeper; my mother-in-law was a teacher, teaching the primary classes of the single school which she ran. And I made this place, so remote from civilisation, which at the time had neither running water nor electricity, my refuge, my chosen place, my haven of peace, my breath of fresh air. And then again, it was my route to a return to nature. It was there that I found other, deeper roots, those of my peasant ancestors. I also understood why I loved to walk about barefoot, to feel the soil, the cool earth, against the soles of my feet. Ever since I experienced the excursions with my father in the Carpathians, I had continued to enjoy these elemental pleasures. My destiny had led me to this place and it is there that I experienced the feeling of a beneficent break with the conformity imposed by the customs of city life, and I could finally behave the way I felt, without constraints. That is what I naïvely told myself. For I was not living there permanently, I merely had the privilege of looting the best part, as a privileged guest, far removed from all the deprivations and difficulties that the village people must have experienced.

From the house of my parents-in-law I had direct access to the river in which I bathed every day. I merely had to cross the road then cut a path across a field of maize in order to find myself on a deserted beach of fine white sand dotted with young birch trees.

At night, I had the impression of coming into direct contact with the stars. On the hill over there, I would chose a tree that I would secretly embrace. On torrid afternoons I would climb the hill behind the house to crunch the black-and-white striped seeds produced by the flat plates of sunflowers. In a few months, I had already absorbed the village customs. I soon felt myself assimilated into peasant life, they considered me to be almost one of their own. On Sunday afternoons, at about four o'clock, I would go and dance the *hora* with the girls, to the sound of a little gypsy *taraf*, a celebration that was held regularly in the school playground, under a leaden sun.

Dating from this period, *ţaţa* Florica imposes herself more precisely in my memories, with the acuity of a lead pencil drawing. She was an Oltenian peasant who had all the attributes of her character – lively, mischievous, cunning and poor as a church mouse. The nickname *ţaţa* means a sort of 'mother so-and-so…'. She was the exact counterpart of Esti, but in a peasant version. That is probably why she left such a marked impression on me, more than any other of the characters who populated the place, because I always considered her as being another Esti. One could say that they were opposite sides of the same coin, each in their way devoted to the same role in the Romanian culinary heritage, in its dual aspects – the country and the city.

As if sketched with the sharp acuity of the pen of a talented humorist, these two women presented, each in their own way, a strong, authentic character, but one that was simplified to the point of caricature. At the same time similar yet different, to see them sitting next to each other was one of the most delicious and amusing spectacles. Both were rather short. Yet while Esti was pale-skinned and plump, a mass of soft curves, *Taţa* Florica was angular, bony, tanned as if desiccated by the sun, the wind and the years of deprivation that she had experienced in her youth. Esti wore her grey hair tied tightly in a bun, with a certain distinction, while *Taţa* Florica covered her tangled hair, in the peasant manner, with a large cotton scarf which she tied under her chin or, when it was hot, at the back of her neck. In the same way, while Esti always wore those short-sleeved dresses of hers, *Taţa* Florica would carefully conceal her scrawny body beneath flowing, long-sleeved dresses, cut from the same dark-coloured cotton or flannelette fabric patterned with flower sprigs; these peasant dresses that reached down to her ankles were designed less to adorn her than to protect her.

Esti, who rarely agreed to travel, was eventually persuaded to spend a few days with us at *Dobriceni*, that little village lost in the Oltenian plain of which she had so often heard us speak so highly. When the day for the departure arrived, she felt as if she were leaving for an expedition to remotest Tibet. She experienced the village as a real culture shock. Having spent part of her youth as a servant among the wealthy bourgeois households of Transylvania, always immaculately presented in her uniform, a little black dress with an embroidered white apron, like a French maid in a farce, Esti did not feel greatly at ease in 'the middle of nowhere', as she considered the countryside to be, exploring it as if it were an unknown world but one which she would approach not without a hint of condescension.

For her part, *Taţa* Florica received her opposite number with a mixture of respect, admiration and yet a hint of caution; for her, Esti's arrival was an event, as it was for the people of the village who had never seen such a creature in their whole lives. Some of them would timidly approach the house so as to be able to study her more closely and give themselves something to gossip about later in the day. For her part, Esti regarded Florica as a peculiar creature. She was not quite sure how to approach her, whether she ought to take her seriously, but somewhere she sensed the toughness and the mysterious strength that emanated from the tiny little woman who was thin as a rake.

Yet despite these hesitant beginnings, they could soon be seen chatting timidly to each other, as they sat on a bench in the sun. They looked like 'the town mouse and the country mouse'.

They began by eyeing each other up and down, like cats sniffing each other, with circumspection and surprise. Having in common the fact that both of them were completely illiterate, Esti, who blossomed like a rose, with her plumpness and her milky white skin, nevertheless dominated *Ţaţa* Florica who saw her as being a 'lady'. Her city talk, spoken in a nasal voice, was a treasured fragment. Pronounced in her slightly jerky Transylvanian accent, such sounds had never come to the uncultured ears of *Ţaţa* Florica. Blackened as a peppercorn, 'raised in the open air', and thus tanned by wind and sun from which she never protected herself, as bent as a comma, she was happy to interject by murmuring her spicy and amusing comments in her frank talk embellished with the Oltenian dialect.

From her earliest days, *Ţaţa* Florica had had a hard life. She had experienced famine, cold, humiliation and even destitution. Her endurance was extreme and she was a stranger to both tears and expressions of sympathy. Despite everything, her innate sense of humour, although of a different type, was very much a match for Esti's and the two of them created a double-act worthy of the funniest stage comedians.

Florica had even more than this in common with Esti. She had been virtually adopted by a family whom she served with devotion, and whom she would never leave. Without ever having married, like Esti, she saw children born one after the other and made them her own. And yet, it is said that when she was very young *Ţaţa* Florica had had a baby that died soon after birth. She never spoke about it.

Once they had become acquainted and they had established what they had in common and their differences, their dialogue became more natural. Esti became used to some extent to the village customs, although always remaining slightly aloof, playing the 'lady' and being treated accordingly in some respects from the outset. She also had certain apprehensions, fears, she was not completely at her ease, she didn't feel at home. Being used to the smooth, clean wooden floors of the flat, she hardly ever left the courtyard which she would cross along a specially laid out route that she had made her own, taking small, hesitant steps and placing her feet carefully on the grass as if she were trying to avoid a trap.

She was unfamiliar with the brilliance of the sunlight and she usually protected herself from it, shading the whiteness of her skin as much as possible in the deliciously cool shade of the orchard. This was the orchard in which my father-in-law, the priest, in addition to his apiculture, devoted himself as an amateur horticulturalist, to strange crosses between species of fruit-trees, which caused him to obtain enormous apples that weighed down the boughs of the trees almost to the ground. We called them 'miracle apples'.

The house in Dobriceni possessed the minimum of conveniences. There were earth-closets at the bottom of the garden as there were in most houses in the country. These were very primitive, consisting of a crude wooden hut in which there was a plain seat in which a hole had been cut, unless they were of the 'Turkish' toilet type. The fact that these toilets were right at the far end of the garden meant that one had to walk about fifty metres to get to them. We noticed that after a few days, Esti regularly refused to eat the watermelon served in the evening at dinner, and would not tell us the reason. We eventually discovered that this juicy food would have forced her to go to the bottom of the garden too often during the night. She was quite simply terrified and was ashamed to admit it to us. We laughed about it for a long time and *ţaţa* Florica, ignoring fear, took advantage of this to make a few sarcastic remarks with her mocking smile about those 'mimsy, stuck-up city women, who are afraid of their own shadow'.

In Dobreceni, *ţaţa* Florica would make delicious, nourishing stews for us, of the type known as *tocană* or *ghiveci*. Esti was visibly jealous, although she tried, not without difficulty, to hide her feelings behind hypocritical compliments that fooled no one. It was here that I had the opportunity to taste a different cuisine, whose genuinely traditional dishes came straight from the Romanian countryside. The delicious stews were cooked in glazed earthenware pots, directly over the embers. The pots were of local manufacture, a craft that I was surprised to learn is very much alive today, thank

God. Such earthenware pots are not supposed to be washed after use, but merely wiped out with a dry cloth, so as to leave them impregnated with the cooking liquids and wonderful fragrances with which they have been imbued over the years. All these foods with their unsophisticated flavours, but which were no less delicious for all that, were cooked in goose fat and even more frequently in lard, which made them a little heavy on the digestion but there were plenty of herbal medicines to remedy this.

That is how the delicious chicken was grilled that melted in the mouth, one of the chickens raised with such care and cruel tenderness by *ţaţa* Florica and which she would call to her with words of endearment accompanied by the usual onomatopaeic sounds to better entice them while they were still alive, while throwing them generous fistfuls of grains of maize. This was only 'all the better to eat them' so that they could subsequently be sacrificed for the benefit of the whole family. That is how I was baptised into that inevitable cruelty connected with the killing of animals. I would declare as being hypocritical any sensitivity I may have had before I went through this 'on the spot' initiation.

The chicken roasted over a wood fire reminded me so much of the chickens that my father used to cook over a spit in the Carpathians. Here, according to traditional Romanian custom, they were eaten with *muşdei*. This was simply a type of uncooked sauce made from a mass of garlic cloves crushed and diluted with a mixture of warm water and coarse salt, which was poured liberally over the chicken while it was still hot. I loved this melting, yet crunchy chicken, thoroughly roasted, even burned in places. The meat exuded the most mouth-watering smells as it came into contact with the garlic whose strength was alleviated by the *mămăligă* at which *ţaţa* Florica was a dab hand.

For it is here in the countryside that the original *mămăligă* is to be found. This is its true home. This is the *mămăligă* of *ţaţa* Florica who stirred it 'in person' and it was no doubt the most 'authentic' of *mămăligă* dishes, the closest to its roots. She stirred as it ought to be stirred, in the old-fashioned way, in a large *ceaun*, a huge cauldron that is passed down from mother to daughter, blackened by decades of cooking. She used a large wooden spoon known as a *făcăleţ*, which, slightly built as she was, she gripped ferociously in both hands, in order to stir it the more thoroughly. One could almost taste how hard she had laboured.

In the summer, after meals, the priest, who liked to cultivate poetry and a certain art of living as if it were a second calling, would present us with the gift of one of his apples. They were the size of a baby's head, round, luminous as a miracle, and he taught us how to munch them using all our teeth, without haste but with a certain religious fervour, to allow us to better experience, he explained, the subtle fragrance and exquisite taste.

At other times, we like to shell green walnuts picked from the branches of a huge tree that shaded our meals in the garden, if the weather was clement. These fresh walnuts had delicate, white flesh like buttermilk. In order to get to it, we had to remove the green skin from the fruit, by crushing it with a large pebble, and this turned our fingers an amber colour that was almost impossible to remove by cleaning, so that we were afraid we would be stained for life. Following the most meticulous operation, peeling the golden skin from the kernels, we finally reached the edible part which was deliciously crunchy.

The night, those nights beneath a huge sky covered in myriads of stars, fell softly. Behind the house, on the hillsides, the tall armies of sunflowers disappeared into the darkness, gradually losing their brightness. We felt ourselves enveloped in a sort of veil that bound us to the trees, the sky, the plants, while the priest's bees slept quietly in their hives.

After dinner, the long night gradually and softly invaded the village and the priest would suggest a walk outside, in the countryside that was illuminated by the milky light of the moon. It was good for the health, he said, it aided the digestion and helped one to sleep better. This ritual stroll before bedtime was only a pretext for long reveries, for whispered conversations and comments about the geometry of the stars. He would talk to us about his youth, his passion for literature, reciting once again whole poems by Minulescu and Blaga, Romanian poets of the inter-war years, whose work he knew by heart.

Furred and feathered game
Twenty-fifth letter to Agnes

How can I describe to you all those smells, tastes, flavours? There will never be enough words to render their scintillating patterns of colour, their infinite variety... Breaking down barriers, allowing these effluvia to invade our five senses, delivering us to this legion of sensations, this avalanche of odours coming from a past that is near or far – or else it was barely yesterday – odours, fragrances, but also the cooking liquids and all those aromas, without forgetting the sounds and above all touch; their obstinate traces move us and awaken in us the memory of the accents of violent nostalgia.

*

There was the şubă, that hunting-jacket lined with hare fur that my father owned. Burying my hands in the softness of that wide opossum fur collar, touching the hares he had killed and that he proudly brandished over my head – no, I wasn't frightened, it was part of life – the soft and silky plumes of the elegant woodcock and wild duck that hung from his hunting bag. Their exquisite colours, their magnificent pelts. On some days I would touch with fascination the cold, hard, dangerous metal of the rifle he cleaned once a month with great ceremony. He would begin by dismantling and unscrewing everything, spreading out each part on the table, itemising the parts of the gun. As meticulous as he was, no gesture was superfluous and he seemed to spend a moment in thought after each stage. As the final stage, he would make the weapon gleam by rubbing it slowly and laboriously with a chamois leather.

On a day that I shall never forget, it was almost nightfall when Father returned from a hunting trip. He would always leave at the end of the week, and I knew he was going to Scurta, a forest somewhere in southern Moldavia, near *Bacău*. He was home and I heard him turning the key in the lock, quietly, as he was in the habit of doing. He came in smelling of the cold, damp air and of fresh game, the smell of a stranger that gave me a slight shiver. The only people in the house were Esti and myself. I was exactly five years old. And Mama was in hospital; I had just been told that she was ill.

I had a strange sensation – something important was happening. As soon as the hall door opened, Esti threw herself forward, she seemed to be in a panic, in a greater state of excitement than usual; she had that fine perspiration that beaded her forehead but she was wearing a sort of smile, the news was good. '*No Conaşu*', *Conaşu*', a little boy' (*Conaşu*' *are un ficior*). So my little brother had been born during the time I had been waiting for my father.

The next day, I was at my mother's bedside with my father; we were dressed in our best and my arms were full of a huge bouquet of orange gladioli. My father told me that my little brother had been born and that we were going to see him at the hospital where my mother was. This seemed to me to be slightly odd; what could be the connection between the birth of my brother and my mother's illness? I found my mother in bed, dressed in a pretty silk nightdress, she was carrying a little packet on her chest that was all red. She looked well and she was smiling. I was rather overcome but lucid all the same; cautiously, I threw an inquisitive eye over the clean, pink hospital room. I wanted to find out how the stork had managed to get in so it could leave my little brother there.

Had I been lied to? For months I had placed a piece of sugar on the window sill and I had even learned a little poem, I would recite it to her endlessly, sometimes I would go and visit the stork where it lived in *Cişmigiu* Park, that's where it was, standing morose, indifferent, dry, perched on one leg. I eventually lost all hope.

The hunt, my father, the birth of my brother. These three elements are linked forever in mind, for no reason except that this specific moment which remains like a tattoo, a sign. He would soon be forced to give up hunting. 'They' had taken it away from him. People told him to sell up, but in vain. He refused to believe it. My mother was angry.

But the habit of eating game in our home remained. Memories, traces in the house at that time – the hide of a hare that I was told my father had tanned himself, the impaled head of a young boar and, of course, the stuffed eagle poised over the Telefunken radio. The eagle which was constantly on the verge of taking flight.

*

Hare was invariably cooked, I don't know why, in the same way, with olives in the so-called Greek-style. This was a family ritual, whose main aspects currently escape me, their memory is very vague, except for the strong, exciting smell, that strong scent of wild animals, that made one go slightly crazy and with which the house was filled while the game was being prepared. It was always an 'event'. Here I am speaking mainly of the time when my father still went hunting hare himself, in Scurta.

My father's role was extremely important; far from confining himself to that of a 'hare-hunter' he would extend it at least to the preliminary stage of preparing the animal, long before it became accessible to our demanding palates and our appetites. This stage, which was protracted and demanding, was anyway considered to be men's work – purist feminists must pardon me this detail – Esti retaining the modest but nevertheless respected role of an assistant, which she performed with an admiring humility and respect for my father.

The most meticulous and difficult part of the work consisted in removing the hide from the inanimate hare, an age-old task that had to be accomplished with a steady and unhesitating hand and which my father performed perfectly due to his long experience. Armed with an impeccably sharpened knife, he undertook this delicate labour every time. I never witnessed the sacrifice, even when I was little, because at such moments the kitchen was strictly forbidden to me; but from what I was able to read later or hear from my mother, I imagine that Esti would hold a receptacle in both hands to recover the blood which ought to have given the scene a character that was loaded with significance, awakening the memory of ancient sacrificial rituals. This blood, more concretely, was mixed with red wine and a profusion of spices and condiments to make a marinade that served as the basis for the succulent sauce. This cruel and blood-thirsty operation was not for the faint-hearted. Mama may well have been one of them for it is only after this that she intervened, that is to say, starting from the actual cooking phase.

At the same time, my father would devote his know-how and skill to dealing with the hare hide. He would rub it vigorously with corn-meal, stretch it out well and nail it to a plank to dry. Later, these skins had become soft and supple and would be stretched out all over the house, simply to be touched, unless they decorated an armchair or cushions or were pushed by our bare heels to the bottom of the bed, mingling quite naturally with the jumble of useless but memorable objects that littered the house.

Presiding over the casseroles, Mama became a queen while the preliminaries have remained in the shadows. The preparation of this dish brought all the members of a family together. I quote the recipe for 'Hare with Olives, Greek-style' as I found it in a work of reference, the *Carte de bucate* by the famous Romanian chef, Nicolae Olexiuc Colea; together with that of Sanda Marin, who was just as well-known, the book has been the cookery bible for generations of Bucharest housewives, teaching them the art of living, in addition to how to prepare food[2].

2. Books by both authors appear in the bibliography on page 191.

Iepure cu măsline
Hare with olives Greek-style

The Marinade

Take two or three onions, half a bunch of celery, a carrot, a few peppercorns and a little freshly ground black pepper, a few bay leaves, thyme, red wine and salt.

The larded pieces of hare are marinated in it for two or three hours or, in the refrigerator, for two or three days.

Hare with Olives

The pieces of meat are then removed from the marinade, wiped dry with a cloth, and lightly fried in a little oil. They are removed from the frying pan and replaced with onions, carrots and a chopped garlic clove. To this are eventually added rabbit's blood, the marinade and some tomato concentrate, after adding the following condiments:

Bay leaf, thyme, pepper, a few tablespoons of vinegar and salt.

Boil the mixture for another hour and pour the sauce over the pieces of meat that have been reserved. Boiled olives, a few slices of lemon and red wine are added, and the mixture left to simmer.

Only at the end are some pearl onions added to the pot.

This exquisite dish is served cold, decorated with fresh parsley and rounds of lemon.

*

Later on, we bought the hare in the market – which sometimes turned out to be a more demanding task than going hunting for it – or someone would give us one as a gift. My father now only rarely went hunting and eventually he stopped going altogether. More often than not, hunting had become the prerogative of the 'bigwigs' the *nomenclatură,* who were in power.

In short Hare with Olives was one of my mother's specialities, her claim to fame. But the well-established reputation of this speciality of our house was due also to a whole group of people, the presentation and the hospitality that our family offered; the good humour and the relaxed atmosphere that pervaded our home were no doubt additional advantages. That is why so many people hoped for an invitation.

On the day on which Mama made hare stew, the whole house was in a turmoil, pervaded by the strong smell of the marinade and we all knew immediately that we would have guests for dinner. Game was always reserved 'for them', a special dish made for a celebration. For the event, the big table was opened out so that it could seat twelve people, never fewer; I still have some recollection of these dinners, at which a whole band of friends would gather, doctors who were colleagues of my mother and engineers who were friends of my father.

On these occasions, Mama would serve what was described with a tinge of irony as 'her posh cooking'. For hors d'oeuvre, there would be a salad of celery with walnuts, or mushrooms stuffed with herbs; before the dessert, as the height of eccentricity for a Romanian dinner, there would be a cheese board. And when I say cheese, the relationship with the richness of the French tradition was minimal, this was a pale shadow of it. There was very little variety, not a trace of either Brie or Camembert, even less of Munster; soft cheeses were not found anywhere on the market at that time, at the very most there might be a slice of Gruyère, rarely some Roquefort and more often a Romanian cheese such as *caşcaval* which has some affinity with cheddar. To such an extent that the very foundation of the meal, the initial wild creature, was transmogrified into a 'civilised hare', a 'creature of the drawing-room'. Everything remained truly delectable, nevertheless, despite these culinary neologisms that verged on heresy.

At the end of the meal, Esti would make a sensational entry by bringing in 'home-made' ice cream. Subsequently, Turkish coffee being consumed at a later hour, the atmosphere became more lively, the laughter and conversation punctuated by witticisms from my father.

Parastas – a Romanian mourning custom
Twenty-sixth letter to Agnes

arastas is a mourning ritual practiced in Romania, first to mark forty days after a death and then again a year later; the most devout extended the custom to each anniversary thereafter.

Yesterday, I was invited to see Gaby, my Romanian friend. She had performed the *parastas* for a dear friend, who had died young a few years ago. The service was held at the Romanian church; on returning to her house, as was the custom, a meal awaited us. The table was already laid with dishes of *gustări* and other hors d'oeuvres which, it goes without saying, were typically Romanian.

She had just returned from Romania, her suitcases filled with *telemea*, *brânză de burduf,* the melting cheese that I have already mentioned that is wrapped in a large piece of pine bark which imbues it with its fragrance, *ţuică*, the local spirit, the large onions they have 'over there' and *leuştean*. Gaby is a true Romanian, who like me is devastated by *dor*, even after so many years.

After the aubergines and the haricot bean purée, the essential starters for a Romanian meal, she served us a good red kidney bean *ciorbă*, well flavoured and full of vegetables; she informed us that it was one of the favourite foods of her dead friend. Then there was a baked *mămăligă* served with the pine-scented cheese and finally, a *plăcintă* filled with pumpkin, the like of which I hadn't tasted in years. Not forgetting the main element in this type of meal, the *colivă*, the dessert made on the occasion of a burial service or in the memory of the dead, so that his soul can rest in peace. This very sweet, thick dessert is made of boiled wheat and a profusion of ground nuts. It is presented on a huge platter, the top being decorated with sweets, sugared almonds and walnut kernels. It is a delight to the diners as well as to children.

At the church or at the cemetery, the *colivă* is eaten as part of the service. It has to be blessed before it is eaten. Members of the deceased's family hold the dish together, at arm's length, while the priest chants the service and leads the congregants in prayers to God for the soul of the departed, asking for his sins to be forgiven. It is a ritual practiced by the Greek Orthodox rite to which we belong.

After the service, a piece of *colivă* is given to those present as well as to the poor who are waiting nearby, knowing what awaits them. At the same time, they are given a small packet of food and they reply with thanks using the word *Bogdaproste*, an old-fashioned term for 'thank you' and then: 'May God keep his soul in peace' or 'May He forgive his sins'. These rituals are known as 'granting the *pomană*'. These words follow the same principle as the term *'de post'* for Lenten dishes. *Pomană* or granting *de pomană* means giving freely out of pure generosity and, paradoxically, rejoicing as well, so that the dead person's sins may be forgiven. But the verb a *pomeni* also means calling someone to mind by mentioning his or her name. The *colivă*, the epicentre of the rite destined to 'care' for the state of the soul of the departed on the other side, unleashes a wave of generosity and, paradoxically, rejoicing, which is in no way considered to be a sacrilege. Thus at this ritual meal there is wine, *ţuică* and an abundance of food. And gradually, a relaxed atmosphere prevails, radiating joy and energy, everyone is satisfied, as if the deceased were still around, circulating among the guests, and one imagines that he or she must be happy, up there, knowing that everyone is talking about him or her. Each person has a story to tell about the dead person's life, people are not just thinking of his or her soul but of him or her, as a person, the way they were when still alive. That is why people eat the deceased's favourite dishes during this meal, with a healthy appetite, without constraints, and everyone feels that this is the way it should be and goes home with a lighter heart, having accomplished a sort of duty to the departed friend.

According to custom, I have put aside a small piece of *colivă* for you, wrapped in a paper napkin, come and taste it when you have a moment, you will like it I am sure. And it will make you think a little about death.

The shared meal
Twenty-seventh letter to Agnes

I take the bus home every evening with all the other 'bureaucrats'. I have never managed to come to terms with this life, that is so unreal, so automatic, I feel it is not my own. Visions of painting are triggered, they pursue me, and run through my head. It's impossible to get rid of them. I will just have to live with them. There is a painting that seems to stick in my mind and yet I know that this evening, like every evening, I still won't get down to painting again. That is how my life is. Dragged down by a host of unimportant tasks, household chores that are drudgery, deceptive, mocking, harassing, are they useful or useless?

Instead of painting, I fill the void by writing. Yes, I write. For the moment, I am writing letters. We'll see what happens later... And then painting is such a cumbersome, fastidious type of occupation; one has to unpack everything, canvases, paintbrushes, tubes of paint, it's too much like hard work... Whereas for writing, a piece of paper and a pencil are all you need, and you can do it almost anywhere. I would say that it is a more worthy occupation, one that is cleaner and more environmentally friendly.

At this very moment I am smiling to myself because, in order to write, on my knees, in the bus, I have rested my piece of paper on the rigid cover of an old book that is beautifully bound as books used to be, covered in lovely marbled paper – published in 1895! – which a dear friend who knows my taste gave me as a birthday present. It is a copy of *La Physiologie du goût* [The Physiology of Taste] by Brillat-Savarin.

Since then, I have used this book as my spiritual guide, my bedside reading, and I would never dare to abandon it.

I find a sensitivity there to which I feel so close, *'Tell me what you eat and I shall tell you who you are'* a phrase that I would even complete with the words 'Tell me how you eat and I will tell you who you are...'; in short, that quality of being able to see beyond the raw materials, to perceive the spiritual dimension of food.

I capture fragments of what I want to reveal, more or less at random, that ineffable part of that which belongs to the table, those poetic moments that are sometimes more than an opulent meal, one that is too perfect; those moments that only survive due to 'everything that was happening around', that indefinable atmosphere that encompasses the 'flesh' of a meal, and which means that one remembers it either as a success or a failure.

*

The taste and quality of food are essential, of course. But here, unlike Brillat-Savarin, what I need to go with my food is not necessarily linked to the *diktats* of classic aesthetics; no, to treat a meal with respect and provide it with the grace and dignity that is its due, I do not require beauty with a capital B, that sometimes frozen perfection which seems to me to be too cerebral, almost tyrannical, which he occasionally describes in his *Meditations*. What I aspire to is the aura floating in the air, consisting of nothingnesses, items of the most minor importance but which come from the soul, the aura that transports us beyond the purely material existence of the food towards a poetic dimension that perpetuates the memory of this ephemeral production and into a warm, unforgettable life experience.

Of course, the presence and choice of guests counts for a great deal, it is a matter of their sensitivity to the good things of the table, their way of communicating with each other, their conversation, their sense of humour – for a meal is above all an act of communion – as well as the spirit of the house, the room in which the meal is eaten, the time of day, the season of the year, and above all the presence and generous disposition of the mistress of the house who knows how to animate the atmosphere; thanks to her presence, her enthusiasm, her wizardry, I would say. A little gesture, a fragment of cloth, the glow of a candle, an anecdote, a gust of laughter, all these are enough to transform even the most modest fare into a memorable occasion.

*

Some occasions may also be failures and it is not so much because the pie has been burned or the *mămăligă* is lumpy or the mayonnaise has curdled – one can always improvise, present it to the diners to the accompaniment of gales of laughter – but because one of the guests has 'cursed' another one, thus spoiling the indispensable harmony; through the presence of these party-poopers, members of an alien race, blind to the pleasures of the table, those sickly, miserable, diet-conscious beings who are ignorant of all the pleasures of life or those who are racked with phobias and prejudices against a particular food. It also happens that the mistress of the house may not be feeling her best and her expression shows the extent of her fatigue, indicating that she has cooked the meal more out of obligation than pleasure and that she is only waiting for one thing, for her guests to leave. All this risks introducing a negative vibration to the gathering from the outset. There is nothing worse than a false note at the start that breaks the spontaneity and has dangerous repercussions throughout the meal. This is how even the most delicious food can lose its very reason for being.

As for me, my dearest, you know me, it is very rare that people of the type mentioned above are to be found at my table. I immediately rule them out.

Romanian Easter
Twenty-eighth letter to Agnes

An air of mild insanity pervades my kitchen. For me, this state of apparent confusion, bordering on despair, is almost a precondition for success and this atmosphere suits me, I feel at ease, at home, it is the natural extension of my state of being. Oh yes, I cannot do without it and I sail gaily through the piles of unwashed dishes and overflowing waste bins. A jumble of pots of ingredients, bottles and flasks clutter the shelves among the cups and glasses. The walls are hung haphazardly with strings of garlic and onions and panoplies of utensils. Everything has been placed in a sort of precarious equilibrium that has something miraculous about it, in this space that is even smaller than the kitchen over which Esti used to preside.

'Tell me, how do you ever find anything in this mess?' the friends who are my guests often tease me, finding my cooking methods to be irresistible, almost comical targets. As for me, I would ask the question the other way round, 'Tell me, how are you able to do anything in this clean, almost perfect kitchen, and keep it that way?'

From time to time, when I feel overcome by vertigo and the chaos turns into something that is almost unbearable, I stop dead. I suddenly find myself tidying up and cleaning as much as possible, even though I know it will never be perfect. And then I start again from scratch.

And then serenity returns, calming even though ephemeral; here I am thus transformed, for an hour or two, into a sensible, calm, reflective person and my movements become more precise. The most simple culinary task, such as slowly peeling an onion, gives me a satisfaction that is close to ecstasy. At such moments, cooking is sublimated into an almost sacred rite; each movement seems to be charged with meaning and to have turned into a ritual. After all, one cannot continue without having a clear out from time to time. But no doubt I also need to lose myself, going to extremes in the opposite direction, balanced on a tightrope.

When I return to oneself, in a calmer atmosphere, favourite moments connected with food return to me, detaching themselves like pearls glinting with a thousand reflections of an infinite richness. It is not only well-established or carefully nurtured cuisine, that which nourishes or that which has been placed on a pedestal, that appears to me; certain details forever embedded in time emerge with just as much intensity. Fleeting images, a particular gesture that has enchanted me forever through the moment that determined it, the tenacious lingering of a scent, a friend who, on a radiant autumn day, in a deserted park flooded with light, presented me with a carefully buttered slice of the freshest bread; the slightly sickening taste of warm milk drawn straight from Lina's goat, and given to me in a dark, damp room a long time ago in *Boiţa*; the acid flavour of a sweet my mother slips into my mouth, in bed, just before I go to sleep; the pacifying sensation of a mouthful of *caş*, that cheese as soft as a baby's thigh; the odour of raw garlic surrounding a chicken roasted in the hearth by *ţaţa* Florica; the strong, acrid smells of game which Elena A. can prepare like no one else in Paris, the atmosphere of an excessive, typically Romanian, generosity that she knows how to create; mornings pervaded with the delicious smell of toast that Mama would eat with her lemon tea; a smell of burning – and here is my father rushing to the kitchen to scrape the dish; my first gulp of red wine when I was three years old and in church, which the priest poured into my mouth from a golden spoon, as if he were a mother bird feeding a chick – it was my first communion; confronting the sea that was so blue, salted Normandy butter at Varengeville; the sweet-and-sour taste of *magiun*, the thick plum jam spread on black bread, as a snack, at *Râmnicu-Sărat*; a huge bacon omelette that a peasant woman agreed to make for us, after long negotiations, somewhere in Transylvania, when we were lost in the countryside with a group of friends, then at Vama Veche on the Black Sea, sardines grilled on a bed of coarse salt, on the beach, devilishly delicious when washed down with *ţuică*. And finally, my favourite moments to be noted down at all costs, the essential, basic foods reduced to their simplest expression, yet which stand out with extraordinary clarity: potatoes grated with sugar and cinnamon; nothing but black bread with walnuts and a glass of wine, and finally, the exquisite simplicity of a hard-boiled egg coloured bright red at Easter, its shell cracking when you bang it against the egg of your neighbour, the joy of exchanging those ritual words: *'Hristos a înviat!'* (Christ is risen!) as the other replies *'Adevărat c-a înviat!'* (He has risen indeed!).

A mixture of impatience and anxiety, impatience to achieve a result extracted from that delicious alchemy, to dip each time into that mixture of smells and splashes of colour from which a dish will result that will satisfy the appetite of the most demanding of diners; anxiety, yes, always, about whether I am up to it, will I disappoint, am I able to reproduce the exact flavour and texture desired, that inimitable flavour, impatient for the moment of deliverance when, slightly out of breath as well as feeling emotional, I will bring out my creation and present it to my friends, my guests, and then before we get down to the meal, we will drink to everyone's health and to the glory of the cooking!

We Romanians belong to a culture of abundance, that of a land full of natural resources, there is no doubt of that. Eating meanly, frugally, mechanically consuming dishes that are inexpressive and boring is almost a sacrilege, it just isn't done. We need the brilliance of vitality, good humour, the feeling of a celebration! Even in a time of austerity and want, we would rather bleed to death than renounce this dimension of joy and delight that transforms all food. It is part of everything and confers upon every successful meal the ample and immeasurable dimension of a celebration. From the outset, there is the giving of oneself. Esti was so well aware of this.

Apotheosis – a naïve painting
Twenty-ninth letter to Agnes

I only have to close my eyes and I can instantly picture the scene, the waking dream of this painting that I shall never complete.

They are there, all three of them. Their image is static only in appearance. An air of perfect happiness prevails under a brilliant light that is not raw or harsh in the slightest. The colours are bright, the contours soft and clear; the impasto is smooth, the brushstrokes of the painting are full and generous.

Mama is on the left, reclining in a totally relaxed position, her back turned slightly towards me, in her rather worn, blue-green velvet armchair, one hand resting on her knees, the other holding a tiny cup of coffee; lost in her daydreams, she smiles with her very blue eyes. Opposite her, my father sits at a little side-table, hunched over as usual, in the process of tinkering with the complicated mechanism of an old fob watch.

In the centre, stands Esti, even more pink-and-white than she was in my memory – one has the impression that her face is like a sponge cake redolent of vanilla – is dressed in a short-sleeved dress. She irradiates a sort of blonde light.

As I contemplate the scene, a miracle happens, she detaches herself lightly from the ground, something that seems to amuse her a little since a smile forms on her lips; she starts rising gently and naturally up to the sky.

Esti appears to be lit from within, a smile of exquisite sweetness illuminates her pale face. As her body lifts into the air, as she rises higher and higher, I have the impression of hearing a whisper of something of her Transylvanian accent, it seems to be the start of a recipe that is barely audible: 'Two eggs, a little flour, a vanilla bean…' but it trails off at the end.

In the background of the canvas, there is a vast landscape with a turquoise-blue sky that is very high above.

In the centre, in the foreground, there is a small, rustic wooden table, on which, clearly visible, there are a smooth aubergine, a few grains of cornmeal, two cloves of garlic and a sprig of dill.

A warm, indefinable, intoxicating perfume wafts from the whole scene. A sharp intensity emanates from it, the characters seem to live in a world apart, engulfed in another time. Yet they appear at ease, more real than they have ever been. I recognise the pure and lively image of this state of grace.

Suddenly, a light shiver shakes this living tableau and I experience a sort of vertigo in my head. The picture frame shrinks at great speed, consumes itself, mutates into a virtual image and speeds off into the distance to disappear into nothingness, like the screen of a television when you switch it off.

So I find myself back in my bedroom, alone, in front of a blank sheet of paper, I prepare myself for another beginning. Very close to my face, by the open window, there is the buzzing of a bee gathering pollen from the geraniums, while a light breeze carries the perfume of the queen-of-the-night flower towards me.

GLOSSARY

The Romanian words in the text have been written in their Romanian spellings. Here are the approximate English pronunciations of the Romanian characters.

a = á
e = é
u = óu
ă = ə The shewa, pronounced 'er' (as in 'mercy', with a silent 'r'), shown in the word list below as ə.
îâ = The glottal stop 'eu' shown in the word list below as y.
ş = sh
ţ = tz

List of Romanian words with their approximate pronounciations.
a face haz de necaz = á fácé haz de necáz
a pomeni = á poméní
Adevărat c-a înviat! = Adévərát c-á ýnviát!
agurida = agourídə
aici zilnic borş proaspăt = aíci zílnic bórsh proáspət
beci = bétchi
bogdaproste = bogdapróstér
boieri = boiéri
Boiţa = Boítza
borş de perişoare = bórsh de périshoáré
borş de potroace = bórsh de potroácé
borşuleţ = borshoulétz
brânză de burduf = brýnzə de bourdóuf
bulion = boulión
burlac = bourlák
Buşteni = Boushténi
cafeluţă = kafélóutzə
caimac = kaimác
caltaboş = kaltabósh

cârciumă = cýrtchiumə
caş = kásh
caşcaval = kashkavál
cămară = kəmárə
căruţă = kəróutzə
ceai rusesc = tcheái rousésk
ceaun = tcheaóun
chiftea = kifteá
chiftele = kiftélé
ciorbă = tchiórbə
ciorbă de lobodă = thciórbə de lóbodə
ciorbiţă = tchiorbítzə
Cişmigiu = Tchishmidgíu
clătite = klətíté
Cocona = Kokóhna
cocoş = kokósh
cofetărie = kofétəríé
colindători = kolindətóri
colinde = kolíndé
colivă = kolívə
compot = kompótt
Conaşu' are un ficior = Konáshou áré oun fitchiór
Coniţa = Conítza
corăbiele = korəbiélé – the Romanian name for it is actually corăbioare
cornuleţe = kornoulétzé
cornuleţe = koviltír
cozonac = kozonák
cozonaci = kozonátchi
damigeana = damidgánə
Domnişora = Domnishóhra
Domnu' (correctly spelled Domnul) = Dómnou
dor = dor
doru' Ancuţei = dórou' Ancóutzéy
dres = dress
dud = doud
dulceaţă = doultchátzə
dulceţurile = doultchétzourilé
esenţa = eséntza
fasole bătută = fasólé bətóutə

făcăleț = fəkəlétz
floricele = floricélé
franzelă = franzélə
frigănele = frigənélé
frișcă = fríshkə
fursecuri = foursékouri
găluște = gəlóushté
ghiveci = ghivétchi
Gicu = Dgícou
gogonele = gogonélé
gogoșari = gogoshári
gogoși = gogóshi
grădina de vară = grədína de várə
grofi = grófi
gustări = gustəri
halviță = halvítzə
hora = hóra
Hristos a înviat! = Hristos á ynviát!
ibric = ibrík
Iedu = Iédoo
iepure cu măsline = iépuré kóu məslíné
Îți mai aduci aminte, Doamnă = Ytzi mai adóutchi amínté Doámnə
kadaif = kadaíf
leuștean = léushteán
macaronari = macaronári
magiun = madgioun
mămăligari = məməligári
mărar = mərár
minciunele = mintchiunélé
mititei = mititéy
murături = mourətóuri
Murfatlar = Mourfatlár
musafiri = moussafíri
musaka = moussaká
mușdei = moushdéy
Ne dați ori nu ne dați = Ne datzi ori nou ne datzi
nenea = nénea
no = noh
nomenclatură = nomenklatóurə
nu mă uita = nou mə uitá

O brad frumos = O brad froumós
Paște murgule iarbă verde = Páshté móurgoulé iárbə vérdé
piftie = piftié
pilaf de dovlecei = piláf de dovlétchéy
pivniță = pívnitzə
plăcintă = plətchíntə
plăcintărie = plətchintəríé
pomană = pománə
porumbielu' cald = poroumbiélou kald
post negru = póst négrou
pridvor = pridvór
pripită = pripítə
Puiu = Póuioo
Râmnicu-Sărat = Rýmniku Sərát
răvașe = rəváshé
salată de vinete = salátə de víneté
saramură = saramóurə
sarmale = sarmálé
sifon = siffón
supiță = soupítzə
ședințe = shedíntzé
șerbet = shérbétt
șpriț = shprítz
șubă = shóubə
tanti = tántee
taraf = taráf
telemea = télémeá
tiribombă = tiribómbə
tocană = tokánə
tochitură = tokitóurə
Tonița = Tonítza
tort de bezea = tort de bezeá
trăsură = trəsóurə
țața = tzátza
țuică = tzúicə
Vama Veche = Váma Véch

186

BIBLIOGRAPHY AND FURTHER READING

Anon, *Romanian recipes*, translated into English by Felicia Marpozan. Bucharest:
The Romanian Cultural Foundation Publishing House, 1999.

Anon., *Savory Romanian Dishes and Choice Wines*:
Bucharest, Publisher Unknown, 1939, updated and republished 1999,
The Romanian Cultural Foundation House.

Balmez, Didi, *Carte de bucate*. Bucharest: Editura Technică, 1978, 1981.

Balmez, Didi, *Rețete culinare*. Bucharest: Editura Technică, 1985.

Colea Nicolae Olexiuc, *Rețetele lui Colea – Preparate din legume fara carne*:
familia marilor nostri artisti bucatari, Editora Teora Verseunea, 2004.

Colea, Nicolae Olexiuc, *Rețetele lui Colea – Carte de bucate*:
supe, ciorbe si borsuri. Editora Teora Verseunea, 2004.

Cristea-Soimu, Maria, *Rețete culinare petru toți*: Bucharest, Editura Technică, 1989

Enache, Dumitru, *Bucătărie pentru toți*. Bucharest: Editura Technică, 1990.

Iosif Hertea, *Romanian carols*. Bucharest, Romania:
The Romanian Cultural Foundation Publishing House, 1999.

Ianco, Ana, *175 Recettes de cuisine roumaine*. Paris, France:
Jacques Grancher, 1990, 2000

Klepper, Nicolae, *Taste Of Romania: Its Cookery and Glimpses of Its History, Folklore,
Art, Literature, and Poetry,* New Hippocrene Original Cookbooks, NY,

Kramarz, Inge, *The Balkan Cookbook*. New York: Crown Publishers, Inc., 1972.

Liess, Martha, *Kochbuch,* Bucharest: Verlag für Fremdssprachige Literatur, 1959.

Marin, Sanda, *Carte de Bucate*, Cartea Romaneasca, first edition, 1938; new edition,
Bucharest: Humanitas, 2006

Marin, Sanda, *Traditional Romanian Cooking,* translated by Alina Deutsch, Black Sea
Publications, Bucharest, 1998

Matei, Cazacu, *The Story of Romanian Gastronomy*, translated by Laura Beldiman,
The Romanian Cultural Foundation Publishing House, Bucharest, 1999,

Mirodan, Vladimir, *The Balkan Cookbook*. Gretna, USA:
Pelican Publishing Company, 1989.

Perl, Lila, *Foods and Festivals of the Danube Lands*. Cleveland, Ohio, USA:
The World Publishing Company, 1969.

Polvay, Marina, *All Along the Danube*, Englewood Cliffs, New Jersey, USA:
Prentice Hall, Inc., 1979; Hippocrene Books (paperback), 2000.

Popoviciu, Nicoleta, *Transylvanian Desserts:
My Mom's Recipes*, Cable, Wyoming, USA: Red Berry Books, 2006

Roman, Radu Anton, *Savoureuse Roumanie*, Montricher, Switzerland:
Les Editions Noir sur Blanc, 2004

Roman, Radu Anton, *Faire la cuisine à la paysanne en Romanie*, Bucharest, Romania:
Editura Padeia, 2007

Sburlan, Smaranda. *Reţete Culinare Pentru Familia Mea*, Bucharest, Romania:
Editura Ceres, 1995.

Septilici, Georgetta, *Gustari Reci...Calde...Salate*, Bucharest, Romania:
Editura Ceres, 1994.

Slăvescu, Micaela, *Cuisine de Roumanie*, Syros-Alternatives:
Paris, France, 1992.

Sperber, Galia, *The Art of Romanian Cooking*, Pelican Publishing Company, Inc,
Gretna, Louisiana, USA, 2002

Stan, Anişoara, *The Romanian Cook Book*, New York: The Citadel Press, 1951.

Printed in the United States
202263BV00001B/196-270/A